*When
blood
flows,
the heart
grows
softer*

—CAMBODIAN
PROVERB

JEANETTE

When blood flows,

the heart grows softer.

TYNDALE
House Publishers, Inc.
Wheaton, Illinois

COVERDALE
House Publishers, Ltd.
Eastbourne, England

Library of Congress Catalog
Card Number 76-8680
ISBN 0-8423-7980-0, paper
Copyright © 1976
Tyndale House Publishers Inc.
Wheaton, Illinois.
All rights reserved
First printing, July 1976
Printed in the
United States of America

For the missionaries
who left their hearts
in Cambodia,
and for their beloved
Khmer people
who amid the tragedy
of war and exile
have found the
Living Jesus.

Contents

Foreword

From the beginning of Protestant missionary endeavor in Cambodia in 1923 until 1970, it was rated as one of the world's most difficult and unyielding mission fields. There was little to relieve the continual heartbreak, dull monotony, struggle, and small results. For almost half a century, there was an incredibly miniscule response. Then, beginning in 1971, came a $4^{1}/_{2}$-year period of miraculous and genuine responsiveness to the gospel. In that short span of time, in Phnom Penh alone, several thousand persons from every stratum of society turned to Christ. Twenty-seven congregations were established and this was largely the work of laymen newly converted.

In order to let the Christian world know of this so unusual movement of the Spirit of God, Mrs. Jeanette Lockerbie was commissioned to write about what God was doing in Cambodia. However, her efforts to enter Cambodia coincided with the rapid deterioration and fall of the Lon Nol government to the Khmer Rouge. She therefore obtained the material for this book by interviewing persons newly evacuated from that sad and war-ravished land. Consequently, the testimonies of salvation, spirituality, good works, zeal, and boldness of several outstanding men in this work of God came to her through their friends and other observers. In God's own time, more information will be learned about the faithful witness of such men as these:

Major Taing Chhirc, educated in France and England
Son Sonne, United Bible Society agent
Minh Voan, M.A. from University of Georgia
Chea Thay Seng, Inspector of Ministry of Culture, holding two degrees from European universities
Pech Bun Nil, Commissioner of National Police
Men Ny Borin, President of the Supreme Court
Nhut Chinda, university professor
Mau Vanna, university professor
Sin Som, schoolteacher

Mrs. Lockerbie has provided a wealth of factual information about Cambodia and God's work in that country. As one would expect from her previous writings, this work has been diligently researched and is presented in a remarkably lucid and readable manner. The book is full of happenings of human interest, all portrayed with "You-Were-There" vividness.

For those who support foreign missions or who wish to become missionaries or study the problems and success of missionary work, it would be difficult to find a more informative and interesting book than this account of missionary durability in the face of monolithic resistance until God crowns the work with massive blessing.

LOUIS L. KING
Vice-President/Overseas Ministries
The Christian and Missionary Alliance

Acknowledgments

I am indebted: To Dr. L. L. King and Rev. T. Grady
Mangham of the Christian & Missionary Alliance for
their willing cooperation in opening to me the files of
the Alliance work in Cambodia. I also greatly
appreciate Dr. King's writing the Foreword for this
book.

To the Rev. and Mrs. Arthur Hammond, the
very first Protestant missionaries in Cambodia.
Mr. Hammond had scrupulously kept a journal, and
he kindly gave me permission to quote from any part
of it.

To the missionaries themselves wherever my
research took me. I could have had little success
without their first accepting me, a total stranger, then
giving of themselves with genuine interest in the
project. To name some would mean leaving others
unnamed. I have to trust that you will read your own

name in this non-list; that you will know I appreciate you and love you. It would be remiss of me, however, to fail to mention the hosts of the C & MA Guest House in Bangkok, Bob and Peg Gunther. Far beyond the call of duty they served me (and the incoming evacuees) during the hectic days we were all their guests. Tirelessly they stretched themselves to provide whatever they possibly could in every situation.

To the Clifford Westergrens of Hong Kong, a heartfelt "thank you" for the store of documented material on Cambodia from which I have gleaned much.

To Miss Gladys Jasper of Evangelical Literature Overseas (ELO), who so efficiently programmed my itinerary that I was free to accomplish what I had set out to do on my missionary writing seminar safari.

To Dr. Ted Engstrom, Mr. Bill Needham, and members of the editorial staff of *World Vision,* for their willing cooperation.

To Mr. Richard Miller, head librarian in Arcadia, California, who offered much assistance and guidance; his interest stemmed from his own years in Cambodia, where he taught English to members of the royal family.

To Dr. Clyde M. Narramore, who showed great understanding when I proposed being gone from my editor's desk for some weeks and then again as I needed time to work on this book.

Finally, to Dr. Victor Oliver of Tyndale House, for asking me to do the book and then for his guidance along the way. And thank you, each one at Tyndale House who has contributed to the production.

Introduction

Why should I presume to write the Cambodia story?

Actually, the assignment was a spinoff from another intriguing project—conducting writing seminars for nationals in a number of Asian countries. Cambodia was my top priority at the time, and because I have an intense interest in missions in general and that part of Asia in particular, Tyndale House Publishers asked me to research and write the Cambodia story.

As my departure date neared, rapid deterioration of the situation made a visit to Cambodia quite uncertain. The response when I inquired about a visa was, "*Cambodia*! Would you like us to issue you a straitjacket along with it?" Nevertheless my hopes were still high. Being a realist, I asked those who were praying that I would get into the country to pray me out again.

My itinerary took me first to Hong Kong, then to

Vientiane, Laos. There, on a Sunday in March 1975, I stood on the banks of the Mekong River. As I gazed at it, my heart pondered all the misery, all the human anguish that river had witnessed in its flow through the delta lands. And I wondered what I would find when again I would meet up with the Mekong in Phnom Penh, Cambodia.

But that was the night my plans changed. With my missionary hosts, Rev. and Mrs. Clement Drager, I went to a dinner at the home of the Australian ambassador and there I had the privilege of meeting and chatting with Mr. Charles Whitehouse, American ambassador to Laos (later appointed to Thailand).

I shared with him that I had not yet been to Cambodia, but that I had information that I could get in. "I'm sure you could go," the ambassador agreed. Then he added with great intensity, "But don't; every additional individual who goes into the country is one more we have to get out." The word pictures he painted left me no doubt as to the cost to others—some U. S. servicemen—whose duty it is to protect the passengers at the prime target, the Pochenchung Airport.

Since diplomatic personnel know more of the situation than I possibly could, I took Ambassador Whitehouse's kindly warning as a piece of God's guidance.

The following day an Air America pilot flying daily between Saigon and Phnom Penh described for me the landings and takeoffs at the Cambodian capital. "No circling for a landing—spiraling down—ducking enemy fire (and being hit once)—taking off at times with the doors still open and desperate people scrambling to get aboard, some dying in the attempt!"

Two seemingly chance meetings. But through them

I felt God was speaking to me.

How then did I obtain this Cambodian story?

It may be trite, but it's nevertheless true that when God closes one door, he always opens others.

How did God do this?

He let me be at the right place at the right time with the right combination of people and circumstances. (Sometimes I feel this is the story of my life; it's exciting and I thank God for it.)

What if I had gone ahead and insisted on spending time in Cambodia? Missionaries who had rightly read the handwriting on the wall were busy making preparations for leaving their work totally under the care and direction of the national church. They didn't need me taking some of their precious hours, sidetracking one of their number to be my interpreter. The Lord knew that and intervened with a better plan, his "Plan A" for me.

As the missionaries evacuated Cambodia, they began to arrive in Bangkok at the Christian & Missionary Alliance Guest House where I was a guest as I conducted a writing seminar for two weeks.

The sadness still on their faces and in their hearts—tears still in the eyes of some—they sat with me and relived their experiences. I can see them yet, a light coming into their eyes as once again they were back in spirit with their beloved Khmer brothers and sisters. It was never an "interview," but a reliving what was uppermost in their hearts. Out of the abundance of their hearts, their lips spoke. Husband would remind wife, "Remember—" and they shared with me. Or, "I'll let my wife tell you this," and the woman's face would reflect her own emotional involvement with those they loved and had left behind.

Breakfast—lunch—dinner; always the evacuees

were there and I began to feel they were all a family and I was graciously made a part of it.

Most of all they wanted to tell me the spectacular things God is doing in Cambodia. I can still hear Gene Hall impressing on me, "It can *never* be past tense, Jeanette. What God is doing in Cambodia is present tense."

I kept running into missionaries from Cambodia in my comings and goings at airports, as well as elsewhere. Others, out of deep interest, made contacts for me. In Hong Kong, for example, on my return from Bangladesh and Bangkok, I was able to meet with *Time* correspondent David Aikman, a warm British Christian brother who shared with me his thinking and insights gained in assignments in Cambodia.

Another "chance encounter," an introduction to a Marine colonel and his wife, led to my spending a day at Camp Pendleton, California. On that occasion, the press officials didn't give me a pass, but a personal escort for the day.

How can I explain what it meant to me to actually meet some of the Christians the very memory of whom had brought a glow to a missionary's face?

And that "delivery room" scene—that sacred moment when a young Cambodian navy ensign said in my hearing, "I want to receive Jesus right now!" This after a harrowing voyage: refused entry at five ports—finally arriving at Camp Pendleton—following some fellow Cambodians into a tent Bible class—hearing the gospel and deciding "the words of Jesus are *truth*"—buying a paperback New Testament—and making an appointment with the missionary to be born again, because "I do not know how to pray to your Jesus."

People ready to accept the Lord: This had become

almost commonplace in Cambodia—after half a century of dismal response to the gospel in that bastion of Buddhism. While rejoicing in the fact that people are turning to Christ in phenomenal numbers, many students of missions are pondering the factors that contributed to this spiritual turnaround.

Why, despite the factors that produced results in other countries, did Cambodia seem so barren for so long?

We can delve for data, we can sift for factors. We can find some answers. But these do not live and breathe; factors and answers do not act and react. People do. And the Cambodian story is one of God's working in and through living, breathing men and women whose hearts the Holy Spirit has touched and who thereafter were willing to follow Jesus—some to the death.

Jeanette Lockerbie
Pasadena, California

Fifty
Years
and
a Dream

Norman Ens wiped the sweat from his face with a gesture of weariness. He couldn't disguise the heaviness he felt as he returned home after a meeting.

"What's the matter, Norm?" his wife asked.

He slumped on a chair, half covered his face with his hands, and shook his head in a kind of despair. "Marie, another eighty prayed to receive the Lord as their Savior."

"And that's what makes you look so sad!"

"Yes," he agreed. "Who is going to shepherd them?"

Every missionary should have such a problem! may be our mental reaction. But this is Cambodia.

It was the summer of 1974. A leading national churchman, Mr. Son Sonne, had asked Ens to sub for him while he attended the International Congress on Evangelization in Lausanne, Switzerland.

Son Sonne had already started five churches, but burdened for an area near his home, he began a Bible study in the home of a new believer. Because swarms of people came around, he had to broaden this into an evangelistic outreach, holding meetings every Saturday and Sunday afternoon.

What was it like those four weeks when Ens substituted for the Cambodian leader?

"We were meeting under a house," Norman explains (the houses are on stilts). "But one house wasn't roomy enough, so the people spilled over under one and then another. I didn't have a PA system, so I was really shouting, because there were quite a few hundred people there. I had decided I would teach one time, then give them an opportunity to accept the Lord, alternating this way. But one time when I closed the meeting after the teaching, they swarmed around me saying, 'But teacher, we came to accept Jesus and you didn't even give us a chance.'

"'Well,' I temporized, 'how about next time? Would that be all right?' But they were so disappointed that 'they didn't have a chance.' I remember that I had to open it up for quite a number to accept the Lord. I've tried to be really cautious about this."

And again, in spite of all Norman Ens' "caution," eighty more had grabbed their "chance." Surely this is a missionary's dream—enough to make him shout, "Hallelujah!" Why then was this missionary of nine years feeling weighed down rather than being on Cloud Nine?

This is Cambodia. Eighty converts in one meeting. And that was just one area. Elsewhere in Phnom Penh and its environs, some twenty church groups were experiencing the same "problem": a runaway spiritual explosion, with little national leadership.

A miracle. And to date the missionaries' experience had not programmed them on "how to handle a miracle."

Who would expect such a thing in Cambodia? Arrogant, Buddhist-dominated, Buddhist-satisfied Cambodia, land of the ancient Khmers.

Half a century earlier, their response to a request from The Christian & Missionary Alliance to enter and preach the gospel was, "There is no place in Cambodia for Christian missionaries. They must never be permitted to enter."[1]

A surprise reversal one year later (1923) was scarcely less negative: "You may preach," the governor grudgingly told Mr. Irwin and Mr. Hammond of the C & MA, "but I assure you *you will have no success.*"

In the succeeding months and years, the government did all in their power to guarantee the accuracy of this governor's prophecy. Everything the missionaries did was challenged. "No" and "You can't" were stock answers to practically every request a missionary made.

"You cannot have a sign on your meeting place."

"You must not proselytize—you must not invite one more Cambodian to your meeting" (sometimes on threat of deportation).

Was this any soil or climate in which to plant the gospel?

Not that these missionaries knuckled under or shrank into the woodwork at each prohibition. They recognized a higher Power and doggedly continued to work and witness. After all, they reminded themselves and each other, Satan is a defeated foe. Nevertheless, each millimeter of progress (this was

[1]From the diary of missionary Arthur Hammond.

then French territory) had to be battled for. It was a dual battle. Every missionary (and, in fact, every Christian) does battle with Satan. But in Cambodia, the Buddhist government was Satan's willing ally.

Are we saying, then, that until the 1970s, Satan and the Khmer Republic were too much for God, that they were totally able to thwart his purpose that all men everywhere (even in Cambodia) might hear and heed the gospel of Jesus Christ?

No. But the dent made in the Buddhist armor by missionaries and their converts was so minuscule as to be nondiscernible to the general populace. Only in the hearts of a handful of believers was there a difference. But God waited. His alarm was set for Cambodia's hour.

Some have speculated as to the effect this "no success" must have had on the early missionaries. This is understandable in our success-oriented, twentieth-century Western society. I probably would have questioned this myself if I had not met some of these missionaries, listened to their experiences, and read the journals they've shared.

In spite of primitive conditions and some less than modern equipment, there was nothing horse-and-buggy about the missionaries in Cambodia. For instance, in 1952 a literature airdrop was successfully carried out. Using the Laos Mission plane and accompanied by the governor of the province, Rev. G. E. Roffe and Rev. Merle Graven flew over the towns and villages of Battambang Province. Rebel activity had made it impossible for either missionaries or national Christians to work there. Many priests joined in the wild scramble for the tracts and booklets that rained down on them in the temple areas, market places, and villages. Later a young Cambodian man from thirty miles away sought out the missionary.

This man carried a soiled and torn tract he had picked up when the drop was made. "I am like the young man in this story," he confessed, "for I am far away from the Father." It was the missionary's privilege to lead the man to Christ, then send him on his way home well equipped with gospel literature to explain the light he had received.[2]

How do you keep on keeping on when it almost seems as if it wouldn't make a whit of difference if you stayed or went?

At every level Buddha was "God." A myriad of pagodas proclaimed it. Saffron-robed priests confirmed it. There was no escaping that entrenched power, nor the enigmatic smile of the Buddha, a patient smile that seems to say, "I'll be here when all others who would oppose me are long forgotten."

All aspects of life revolved around the temples: social life and customs, education (the schools were on the temple grounds), economics, politics, as well as religion. Every influence emanated from the Buddhist temple, from belief in Buddha. The glories of the nation's past were their famed temples. Their life after death hinged totally (according to their culture) upon their obedience to Buddhist principles.

How then could two, later four, then a dribble of foreign missionaries with a foreigner's religion hope to penetrate this fortress of heathenism?

Lesser souls than these first missionaries and those who followed them in the early days would have taken the first boat home.

Often, even the prospects that looked hopeful ended in disappointment. Mr. Hammond tells of a trip that took them overnight on a crowded river

---

[2]*Light in Their Dwellings: A History of Forty Years of Missions in Cambodia,* compiled by C & MA's *Cambodia* news staff, 1962, p. 38.

boat, complete with bedbugs, to evangelize and distribute literature. En route they met a man who showed great interest and Mr. Hammond explained what the books were about, talking with the man for about an hour.

"Will you come to my village and tell the people what you have just told me?" Mr. Nou asked. He took Mr. and Mrs. Hammond in his motor boat and stopped along the way, where a village chief treated him with great respect and called all the people in his village to hear what the Americans had to say. The people gathered and Mr. Nou commanded them to stand quietly while Mr. Hammond told them about the true God.

"When we arrived at Mr. Nou's village," relates Hammond, "we could see by his house that here was a wealthy man. After a good French meal, he took us and showed us the source of his wealth. He had a modern sawmill (in those days most lumber was sawed by hand). As we passed through the mill, he gave orders for everyone to go out in front of his house. There were fifty or sixty people standing below the veranda. Mr. Nou said, 'There they are. Preach to them.' So for nearly an hour I told them the gospel story and presented Christ to them as the only Savior, who died for our sins and rose again from the dead and is alive at the right hand of God the Father.

"There were absolutely no results of these meetings; never an opportunity to follow up with visits to the individual homes. Many people in Cambodia have heard the gospel in this way, but Buddhism has been their way of life. They have never known any other way than to obey everything that Buddha commanded, believing that this gives them a fair chance for their next existence. From childhood they are taught never to desire anything else.

"But I was intrigued by this Mr. Nou, so anxious to have all these people under him hear the gospel! Surely he would believe! But when I tried to get him to accept the Lord Jesus as his Savior, he responded, 'I know it will make them better people, *but it is not for me.*'

"No argument could change his mind. Reluctantly we took the next steamer that came down the river, saddened that not even one person had turned to Christ."

What kept the missionaries from quitting? (Naturally, a lot would depend on the individual and his own dynamics.)

These first missionaries were not supermen, not superwomen. They were, to be sure, trained and called to their work. But so were others who in similar circumstances either figuratively or literally "shook the dust off their feet" and moved on to more fruitful pastures. But apparently neither slim pickings nor open hostility deterred the missionaries in Cambodia.

Could it be that the work itself, their commitment to specific tasks, is the clue as to why they didn't give up (if the thought ever occurred to them). How, for instance, can you quit in the middle of a chapter you're translating when there's no one else to do it; when it's the Bible you're translating, a Bible the people have never been able to read in their own language?

That was Mr. Hammond's position. Probably there were plenty of times when he would have been glad to get out from under the pressures. No dictionary in the language. No defined spelling of the words with which he was dealing. "Helpers" who professed to accept the Christian religion that was giving them a job, a claim to faith that lasted just as long as the job itself. Add to this the enervating heat, "the awful sameness of it," wrote Mr. Hammond. In Clifford Westergren's years in Cambodia, he attributed the low motivation of the average Cambodian to this extremely hot climate.

"My language informant could be compared to a sponge," says Mr. Hammond. "Pressed for information, he gave it out; but after two or three squeezes he was dry. He was quite good at teaching the characters and phonetics but when it came to the meaning of words, everything was just either 'good' or 'bad.'"

For eight months, alone, Arthur and Esther Hammond plugged on. Then the Ellisons arrived to pioneer in Battambang.

For twelve years, as others joined the skeleton crew, they were all kept under the thumb of the Surete (Secret Police). Visas were necessary for inter-city travel and the missionaries had to report to the Surete before they could travel. "For your own protection," was the explanation.

Notwithstanding the surveillance and harassment, the missionaries saw some, not many, Cambodians turning to Christ from Buddhism.

When the authorities found the missionaries hard to discourage, they tried another tack: "You must give a list of the names of converts to the Surete," they insisted. And when the missionary went to visit a convert again, he was nowhere to be found, undoubtedly intimidated by the Secret Police.

Another repressive threat would have terminated all missionary endeavor in that country. An SOS for prayer was signaled to a few in the homeland who had committed themselves to pray for Cambodia. How did God answer? The official who had issued the threat and who had power to enforce his edict, suddenly left the country. It wasn't his health. It wasn't a political move. Nor was it a promotion. He couldn't stand the climate. (We might ponder why he had been able to tolerate the climate until people started praying.)

The pressures against the missionaries eased some with the exit of the hostile official. But the going was still uphill all the way, and from a human perspective, unrewarding.

It would be a gross understatement to say that these missionaries were never statistic-happy over the results of their efforts; their letters home and their reports to the home board didn't elicit hallelujahs. But what if Arthur Hammond had not persisted in his translation of the Bible? To be sure, he took up the matter with the immediate intent of improving his knowledge of the Cambodian language, which he had studied while waiting to enter the country. He had no congregation to greet him in Phnom Penh. No former missionary had left a nucleus of Christians who just needed nurturing and guidance, then they would pick up the ball and carry it. No such thing. He had to make his own wedge in the door with opposition all the way.

"No success" is all the harder to take when your nearest missionary neighbors are reveling in Book of Acts experiences, as were the C & MA missionaries in nearby Viet Nam. In 1916 Dr. Jaffrey was granted official authorization to do Christian work in Haiphong, Hanoi, and Tourane (Da Nang), and with no "You will have no success" clause attached. There wasn't a mad rush of people eager to hear the gospel of Jesus Christ in Viet Nam. The missionaries had a slow start, then came World War I to curtail their activities. But by 1917, eighteen had been baptized and from that time on, the work grew. In each of the principal cities, the beginnings of the Lord's work reads like a continuation of the Book of Acts.

The Holy Spirit brought key men and women into contact with the missionaries. In Hanoi, a celebrated sculptor, and the editor of the newspaper, as well as a wealthy university man; in Tourane, the wife of a duke at the royal court of Hue, a Confucian classical scholar of reputation, four members of the Annamese royal family, and three customs officials: these and other influential persons comprised the nucleus. The Tourane church doubled its membership each year until there were over 1000 members. The Christians had received the contagious type of salvation and as in the days of the apostles, they went everywhere gossiping the gospel. One believer, a popular actor, was converted, trained in the Bible school, and became a famous preacher. Like Paul, he was jailed because of his phenomenal success (1000 converts in one year) and brought before the governor, who released him and later told a missionary, "He almost persuaded me to become a Christian."

Viet Nam, yes.

Cambodia? Not yet.

Things *were* happening. Not spectacular, but can anything be of more long-range, vital importance than a translation of the Scriptures? The production of that first Bible is a story in itself. I've heard, for instance, of the "much traveled type" that was ultimately hand set by student volunteers at Nyack, one of them Clifford Westergren who would later head up the Alliance Press in Phnom Penh (now directing the Press in Hong Kong).

The day came when a beautifully bound special copy of the Cambodian Bible was presented to His Majesty King Norodom Sihanouk, a presentation made by Rev. Curwen Smith of the Bible Society and Rev. David Ellison, mission chairman. Much impressed, the king asked who had done the translation, how long it had taken, and where it had been printed and bound. It has been reported that later, when the king was asked to judge a member of his government who had embraced Christianity, he said, "What this man believes is between him and myself. In fact, I have the Christian Bible and I read it every day."

How far, we might ask, would the converts of the seventies go and grow without the Bible in their own language?

Significantly, one of the miracles of 1975 is that in the very last convoy of supplies to reach Phnom Penh by river was a shipment of newly printed editions of Cambodian Bibles, Testaments, and Gospel portions. "What a miracle," wrote Ted and Marjorie Cline of the United Bible Society, "that the barge containing these tons of Scriptures was one of two that arrived safely in Phnom Penh."

The world press was keeping score of the supply ships that sank and the pitifully few that survived the enemy fire on the Mekong. Meanwhile God was keeping his watchful eye on those Bibles.

A Bible made possible because a missionary wouldn't quit.

And what of the Bible school? By 1925, the Ellisons had a school under way with five men students. After one year of study, four of these were assigned to practical work and distribution of the Christian literature then being published.

Did these few students and the ones who followed become the seed sowers of the present spiritual harvest? Was God waiting for it to germinate?

In their own time these students made sufficient

ripples that the government took notice. Officials ordered Rev. Ellison to appear at the office of the French Administrator. There they accused the missionary of carrying on work without authorization and of conducting a "clandestine school." All phases of missionary work were ordered to be stopped immediately under threat of deportation.

Another "You can't."

Another special plea for prayer. This time God's way of countermanding the order was through a loophole in a previous administration!

The Bible school, successively administered by the founding Ellisons, the Sechrists, the Taylors, the Gravens, and the Paul Ellisons (second generation missionary), is one of the most encouraging arms of the work in Cambodia. During Rev. Merle Graven's tenure, he was concerned that the national believers catch a vision of missions for themselves. He had called a Youth Committee to discuss this matter and before he could make any suggestions one of the young men students interrupted, saying, "Excuse me, sir, but I must tell you what happened last night. I was praying and I heard the voice of the Lord speaking to me, asking if I would spend my long vacation this year up in the Tribes' area. I knew I had to go. I didn't think about how I would get there. I didn't know how I would live after I got there. I didn't know whether the church committee would send me or not. I only knew I had to go because God had called!"

And at the suggestion of Merle Graven the various youth groups through their offerings supported their own missionary for three months as he took the gospel to the tribal people in his own country.

Meanwhile God had a special bonus for Mr. Hammond. He finally was blessed with a translator who knew what he was doing and was conscientious about his work. Writes Hammond, "He wasn't the kind who has to stop for a drink of water or a cigarette every half hour. So I was a little surprised when one day he came tapping at my study door. Then I became more intrigued with his manner as he stood trying to find a way to say what was on his mind. When Cambodians are nervous or embarrassed, they stand on one foot, then the other, cracking their knuckles; the way they do it, it makes quite a noise.

"Why was he so nervous? I asked myself, as his fingers crackled like a bunch of firecrackers. Did he want a loan on his salary? Was he trying to ask for a vacation, or what? Maybe he was going to say that unless he got a raise in pay, he would quit. Almost immediately," recalls the missionary, "I was sorry for what I had been thinking, for what did this man, Ham, want? What had brought him at such great discomfiture to himself?

"'*Loke* (Mr.),' he began, 'I take this book you gave me home to study for the morrow. I read a good portion of it and study the words and expressions in it. It is all so interesting I just cannot put the book down. I read on and on. My wife gets angry with me, that I don't put out the lamp and go to bed. But I can't help it. I read and read, sometimes 'til midnight. Now I have finished the whole book, and I am persuaded that this Jesus you talk about when you explain things to me, is the true God and I now want to become a Christian.'"

Mr. Hammond didn't think this man needed more knowledge before accepting Christ as his Savior. What was necessary, however, was that he understand what it would cost for him to become a Christian; that he would undoubtedly be ostracized by his friends, mocked by many of them; he might even be put out of his home, for he would be one of a very, very few Christians in Cambodia at that time.

Ham responded by saying he had already written his parents and told them of his desire. They had replied that he was old enough to know what was right, and he had their permission. As far as his friends and intimate associates were concerned, he wasn't afraid. He wanted to be a Christian.

From the time he received the Lord, it was very evident that the Holy Spirit had opened up Ham's mind. Prior to this time, as he and Mr. Hammond worked together, they read aloud the portion they would be working on that day, then reread a verse at a time and dissected it, studied it, and discussed it in relation to the context, until Ham came up with something in Cambodian that would match its meaning. Sometimes a whole morning would be spent searching for the exact right word to translate it. But the day following his conversion, after the preliminary reading, he was ready with the right words and formation of sentences. It was hard to believe he was not faking, but careful examination of everything Ham had written proved that the Lord had given him spiritual insight beyond their expectation. From that time on, instead of a few verses a day, they would finish a couple of chapters (depending on their length).

What was true of this early translator has been strikingly true of the converts of the 70s: A remarkable spiritual comprehension right from the day of conversion appears to have characterized these Cambodian believers. Surely this is the work of the Holy Spirit for his particular purpose.

Jesus said, "I will build my church." And as only he can, he was selecting living stones, so Cambodia would be a part of his church. Some of us, locked into our own pattern and procedure, might raise our eyebrows at the Holy Spirit's methods—but they work!

An old woman dreamed of a tall man who came into her village with a pack of books on his back, and she was told to buy some of these books and believe what was written in them. Cambodians take great stock in dreams. They are recounted to the elders for their interpretation, but this woman's dream was a mystery to them. She never forgot it, however.

One day after the missionaries had started producing literature, a colporteur, a tall Vietnamese, came to her village. She heard her neighbors running and excited voices outside, so she looked to see what was happening. As she saw the crowd gathering, her gaze rested on the tall man who was the cause of the excitement. He was talking about books and selling them to the people. She let out a cry, "That's the man I saw in my dream," and she sent one of her sons to buy some books. Then she sat in her home and read them to her family. "We must believe these books," she told them, "for that was commanded me in the dream."

The outcome was that the missionaries, after an arduous river journey (on which they prayed, "Lord, we thank thee for this food; please protect us from it") visited that village. A number of the people accepted Christ and some went on to Battambang Bible School.

Then there was the ferry pilot who became known as "Mr. Jesus" because he was always talking about the Lord and what he had done for him.

Still another of the Holy Spirit's handpicked trophies was the former monk, Li, who to try to ease his burden of sin went from teacher to teacher, always hoping that the next one would have the answer for his heart's unrest. One day a traveling colporteur came to Li's village and went door to door selling books. It was during the heat of the day and when this man arrived at Li's house, Li was resting. The colporteur stood at the foot of the ladder leading up to the front door of the house, up on stilts, and shouted, "Does anyone in this house want to buy a book that tells about the true and living God, the one who takes away sin?"

Hearing this, Li jumped up and hurriedly called the man up into his house. He kept him there for two or three days until the colporteur had shared the gospel with him and had explained all that the missionaries had taught him. Before leaving, the colporteur led Li to Christ. At last his burden of sin was gone! Many are the tales of his witness and service to Christ the rest of his life.

Can any evidence of the witness of these first converts be pinpointed today? Are there some who can trace their spiritual ancestry back a few generations?

Ask one of the leading laymen in Cambodia today, Major Thaing Chhirc, a third-generation Christian. His grandfather, the first in the family to be reached with the gospel, heard only a few words. "Worship the true God," a convert from Buddhism, Daraith, told him. He believed, turned from Buddhism, and brought up his family so effectively for Christ that his grandson is a noted Christian. You will meet him from chapter to chapter.

After forty years of missions in Cambodia, the missionaries there at that time stated their desire, "To work ourselves out of a job." They shared this concept and elaborated on it in these words:

We had a dream. The missionaries had left

Cambodia. Their houses were empty, their
vehicles gone. But the reason for their departure
was not war or bad deportment. Rather, they
were no longer needed. No longer needed? The
church had come alive! Her seed which seemed
to have been sterile for forty years was bearing
spiritual children. For the first time, the Bible
school considered whom to reject because of
crowded conditions. The problems which long
had stunted her growth and muffled her voice
were missing. Relentless preaching which broke
men under its force, combined with due respect
for all the servants of the Lord, was
unprecedented. The influence of her message
could not be ignored. The largest group
responding was the students, the Cambodia of
tomorrow. Within her own ranks, the church's
two outstanding marks were holy living and
missionary vision. These qualities rubbed off on
everyone coming close enough. The vision of the
tribes and the Cham (Muslim) people gripped
hearts. The church had come alive! But this is
more than a dream. It is the throbbing
expectation that out of Cambodia's unyielding
soil of Buddhism will soon leap forth a candid,
vibrant, spotless church.[3]

A dream. A dream come true.

A Cambodian layman attending a world congress on
evangelism. A missionary temporarily taking this
Cambodian's place, and because the soil is right,
because the seed has been sown—eighty converts in
one meeting.

Who will shepherd them?

[3] *Ibid.*

Not many days were to elapse before the missionary would have even greater cause for concern over these Khmer Christians.

Who Are These Khmers?

Historically, crisis countries come into the public consciousness. The seventies have seen this in abundance—Biafra and Bangladesh, to name just two. Raw human horror has earned screaming headlines in the world press.

Less space and sustained emphasis has been given Cambodia, the Khmer Republic. Nevertheless, this country, too, due to war, refugees, and finally Communist takeover, has gained the attention of people who previously didn't even know which continent hosts Cambodia.

What has not received much publicity is the richness of this nation's heritage.

This book makes no claim to deal with the history, geography, and politics of Cambodia, but we do need some background to understand who these Khmers are and what makes them what they are.

If conditions were to permit the Khmer people to have a national birthday party, they probably would not know how many candles to light. Martin F. Herz writes:

> The origins of Cambodia are shrouded in mystery. Legend has it that an exiled Indian prince once came to its shores, where he fell in love with the daughter of the Snake King, married her, and founded a dynasty. There is some faint historical evidence that this prince may have been identified with a Brahman noble by the name of Kaundinya who is mentioned in Chinese accounts of a country called Funan, which is the predecessor of Cambodia . . . The union of the King and a snake goddess constitutes a central theme of Cambodian mythology, and the seven-headed snake or *Naga* is found depicted throughout the art of the country of Cambodia.

(I've heard hints as I've talked with various people who lived in Cambodia that there is a vague belief that the Garden of Eden was on the delta of the Mekong!)

"It is from the writings of Chinese who came to trade—writings that became part of later Chinese histories—that we glean most of what we know about Funan," wrote Mr. Herz.[1]

At the height of its power, the Khmer empire encompassed all that part of Southeast Asia now known as Cambodia, Laos, Thailand, and Viet Nam. The sixth to the fourteenth century was its golden age, and there is abundant evidence of their early,

---

[1]Martin F. Herz, *A Short History of Cambodia* (New York: Frederick A. Praeger, 1958), pp. 8, 9.

highly advanced civilization. Cambodia was the center
of this empire that in the twelfth century extended
from the Bay of Bengal to the China Sea.

Judging by the area included within the
surrounding wall, the royal city, Angkor, lost to
civilization for centuries, could easily have contained a
million inhabitants.

In an intensely fascinating article that portrays the
glories of the ancient Khmers, W. Robert Moore,
Chief of the Foreign Editorial Staff of *National
Geographic Magazine,* writes:

> A century ago a French naturalist named Henri
> Mouhot, exploring in remote Cambodia, heard
> tales of a fabulous "lost city" in the jungle.
> Skeptical but curious, he persuaded a local
> missionary to guide him to it. They traveled first
> by canoe and then afoot. Finally, breaking
> through the bush, Mouhot saw the ruins of what
> we now know as Angkor.
>
> Great stone temples stood strangled by vines.
> Massive gateways, carved walls, and ornate
> terraces lay overgrown by gigantic silk cotton
> trees and tentacled banyans. But there were no
> people! Only the cries of birds disturbed the
> solitude as he prowled the tumbled stones and
> marveled at the eerie ruins.
>
> Because it was so overgrown, Mouhot could
> not realize at first the full magnificence of the
> metropolis he had come upon: scores of temples,
> miles of roads, an intricate network of canals,
> causeways, moats, and reservoirs.
>
> What unknown people had built it?
> Why had they deserted it?
> When had they left?
> When Mouhot, amazed and baffled, asked

these questions of Cambodians living nearby, they could tell him little.

"It is the work of Pra-Eun, the king of the angels," they would say, or "It is the work of the giants"; or even "It made itself."

When I [Moore] asked a weathered old pilgrim, "Who built it?" I got almost the same answer Mouhot had received a century earlier: "The gods," he answered. "Only the gods could do so much!"[2]

This last quote ties in with the analysis of author Malcolm McDonald when he states: "Religion is the strongest impulse of their [the Cambodians'] lives."[3]

Magnificent photography in the *National Geographic Magazine* article illustrates the almost incredible art, culture, and architecture of these fabulous Khmers. To this day it cannot be determined by what technological process they hauled the enormous blocks—some weighing as much as four tons—from Phnom Koulen, some fifty miles distant, and how they hoisted them into place.

One of the reservoirs in their irrigation system measured one kilometer (about five-eighths of a mile) by two. (In 1958, with American aid, this was being reconstructed after 500 years).

Though nothing is known of their medicine, it is known that they had 102 hospitals.

Their astronomers could calculate the eclipses of the sun and moon.

Scribes used a kind of chalk on black-colored deerskins or parchments.

Agriculture was highly developed; the renewal of

[2]W. Robert Moore, "Angkor, Jewel of the Jungle," *National Geographic Magazine,* April 1960.
[3]Malcolm McDonald, *Angkor* (New York: Frederick A. Praeger, n.d.).

the soil due to the annual flooding of the Great Lake produced four crops a year.

There is no question but that the Khmers had, in early times, reached the heights. But, as Malcolm McDonald points out,

"It always takes much longer to climb uphill than to run down."

Decadence set in.

The once mighty empire was whittled away by a succession of wars with predatory neighbors. Some have seen the Cambodians' relationships with their neighbors in surrounding countries as something of a parallel with the historic Israel/Arab situation. It's not a twentieth-century problem, nor will it be easily solved.

When French colonialism penetrated that corner of Asia in the nineteenth century, Cambodia was a far cry from the splendor of the god-kings Yasovarman and Jayavarman VII, the builders of the fabled Angkor temple cities.

There was little resistance to the French until World War II. The hand of French colonialism rested lightly on Cambodia, maintaining the monarch in a splendor unseen since the Angkorian era and doing nothing to disturb the tranquility of the country.

Nationalism stirred in the 1930s and France's plight in World War II added to its impact. On the death of King Monivong in 1941, the French bypassed his son and heir and elevated to the throne 18-year-old Prince Norodom Sihanouk. Within a few years the young ruler was embroiled in political struggles—the pangs of Cambodia's rebirth as a sovereign nation—that again rocked the country in the brutal convulsion of the 1970s.

The French had considered Sihanouk to be a compliant youth. But far from being a puppet, "the people's Prince" had been cautiously moving toward independence. With the granting of independence in November 1953, having assumed full powers, Sihanouk embarked on programs to combat illiteracy and disease in the countryside and to add to his nation's budding industrial capacity.

Feeling limited and confined by his royal role, in a surprise move on March 2, 1955, he abdicated his throne. He had needed the authority of the monarch to carry forward his struggles for independence. As king he was the recognized voice of the people. Now that sovereignty had been achieved, however, Prince Sihanouk wished to be free of the trappings and the demands of a court; to be, in truth, "the people's Prince," having access to them and they to him. He wanted to come to the aid of the "little people" and ease their lot in life.

He did accede to the request of the National Assembly to become Head of State, some three months later, when still there was no king on the throne.

Would not this self-sacrificing love, this demonstrated concern for his people, explain their later disenchantment, the hollow disillusionment of the hero-king followers?

"Our king left us," was their mournful lament.

Not only was the king their protector, but in the Cambodian mind he was a kind of god-king, Buddha being the "god."[4]

The story is told that on one occasion, when King Sihanouk was touring a remote area, a whole series of catastrophes were plaguing the peasantry. Bandits terrorizing the district—jungle animals marauding the

[4]Factual editorial on Sihanouk from Hong Kong *Standard*, April 18, 1975, p. 8.

crops—and the weather adding its own disastrous
effects. The simple country people turned to their
king and asked him to stop all these things.

When Sihanouk insisted that he had no control
over such things, the people looked incredulous.

"But you are our *king!*"

"Yes," said Sihanouk, "I am the king, but I'm just
a man."

The people could not comprehend this. To them
their king was at least part divine.

To have any understanding of Cambodia it's
necessary to fully realize that fact and something of
what makes a devout Buddhist tick.

Men knowledgable in the thinking processes of
Asian peoples deplore it that those in the West
formulating policies concerning Asia, do so with no
knowledge or awareness of the differences between
them, the deep philosophical differences.

Jerrold Schecter, in *The New Face of Buddha*[5]
writes:

> Buddhism in Asia is basic belief and bedrock
> identity; it influences power, sex, psychology and
> economics. Buddhism is not only religion and
> philosophy; it is also nationalism and ideology, it
> is the ultimate source of Asian values. Yet it is
> an area in which the West is woefully ignorant.
>
> Just as the Greco-Roman and Judeo-Christian
> traditions are the basis for political thought and
> behavior in the West, Buddhism is the resource
> of power in the East. There is in Buddhism a
> complete way of thought, uniquely Asian, which
> explains man to himself in the mirror of eternity.
>
> In the cities of Southeast Asia, education and

[5]Jerrold Schecter, *The New Face of Buddha* (New York: Coward, McCann,
and Geoghegan, 1967), pp. 11, 16 (Introduction).

economic aid have provided a common facade for talk and socialization between Asian and Westerner, but rarely for psychological insight or understanding. Westerners are outsiders. Western wealth and power are respected or scorned, often coveted, but rarely understood. Beside the obvious differences in race and economic development looms the most deep-rooted psychological difference of how man approaches his deity—the concept of God. The vastly different mystery of Asian belief in the infinite affects the passions and actions of Asian life and plays a crucial role in the economics and politics of the Buddhist countries of Asia.

As far as religion is concerned, nothing changed with a 1970 coup that deposed Sihanouk and brought Lon Nol to power as president of Cambodia. The text of Lon Nol's "Message to Buddhist Believers"[6] contained such items as:

. . . According to an oracle, the current war in Cambodia is a religious war . . .

"I wish to inform my fellow countrymen who are Buddhist believers that an oracle has predicted that everybody will enjoy equal rights. Everybody will be happy and good when this religious war ends. But while the war is going on, you must respect your religion and pray. Those who follow that advice will be spared all misfortune and will be rewarded with security and prosperity . . .

"When the war ends, Cambodia will become a Khmer republic. Democratic power will be put

[6]Jonathan S. Grant, Lawrence A. G. Moss, and Jonathan Unger, *Cambodia, The Widening War in Indochina* (New York: Washington Square Press, 1971).

in the hands of the people . . . there will be no
longer a king"—and much more of the same
predicting victory for the Buddhists against their
"religious enemies."

Until April 1975, then, it could be said
unequivocally that Cambodia was Buddhist all the
way. Over the centuries, like a lazy octopus slowly
wrapping its tentacles around the masses, Buddhism
has engulfed the people. At every turn, temples and
pagodas met the eye. Ornate, gold-decorated, they
gleamed in the hot sun. Even the smallest village has
its pagodas. Interestingly, Buddhist temples are for
housing the gods and offering sacrifices, not places of
worship in the sense that our Christian churches are.

Every day begins with the procession of
saffron-robed monks making their way, single file,
begging bowls in hand for their alms from the
faithful.

Each family gives a son, at least for a time, to the
temple.

There is a ministry of cults in the national
government and the entire religious system is highly
organized.

Understandably, a foreign religion met with almost
insurmountable barriers.

The first attempt to scale these walls of Buddhism
was by some Portuguese Catholic fathers who arrived
in 1553. These were followed by Spanish and later by
French priests. But though Catholic missions have
been conducted in Cambodia for more than four
hundred years, they have met with little success in
converting Buddhists.

For centuries, Protestant missionaries were rigidly
excluded though several missionary societies sought to
gain entrance. The king desired no importation of

foreign religions. Even after becoming a Protectorate of France, the nation remained exclusively Buddhist. The French government, preferring to keep it so, forbade missionaries to enter.

But, as we have seen earlier, in February 1923 the Christian and Missionary Alliance was permitted to open a station in Phnom Penh.

The C & MA's Foreign Secretary, Dr. L. L. King, chronicling their work in Southeast Asia, underscored what we have already noted in Chapter 1, the brick wall of resistance they encountered: "When missionary work was initiated in Cambodia, the third largest Alliance field, failure was freely predicted. But Cambodians *have* been converted, and their lives are testimonies to the fact that the gospel is still the power of God unto salvation. Yet, considering the total population of Cambodia, the response has been disappointing. Buddhism binds the people and makes the presentation of the gospel difficult."

Modern Cambodia lies west of the Vietnamese mountain chain. It is bounded on the south and east by Viet Nam, on the north by Laos and Thailand, on the west by Thailand, and on the southwest by the Gulf of Siam. The area is 66,590 square miles, about equal to that of the states of New York and Ohio.

The approximate seven million population of modern Cambodia is largely rural, with agriculture the chief means of livelihood. Rice, grown on three out of four acres of cultivated land, constitutes 90 percent of the average diet; its processing, transport, and marketing afford employment and support the economy.

The Cambodian people have a rural frame of reference; their characteristics are largely those of a farm people. The second sparsest population in Asia, they have as a group had more food than other

Asians. Overpopulation with its attendant hunger has not been a problem for the Cambodian; adequate natural resources have met their simple needs. Therefore, the sudden hunger of the war refugees was something for which they were totally unprepared. Thus the trauma was that much greater.

Racially, the Cambodian is more akin to India than (as his Vietnamese neighbor) to China. The Cambodian does not have the epicanthic fold (slant) eyes. He resembles the Filipino. To illustrate, missionary Clifford Westergren recalls once when a Christian visitor from the Philippines was immediately surrounded by the friendly church members; they greeted him in Cambodian, as one of themselves.

Through racial intermarriage, however, Cambodians are as varied as Americans. They range in color from the swarthy French-Cambodian and yellow Sino-Cambodian through shades of brown to a near-black of the Indian, Malay, and Negroid types. Their physique also differs widely according to racial ancestry.

A strong trait is the Cambodian's love for his language. They resisted the Roman script, retaining their beautiful Sanscrit-based written characters.

Literacy has never been a problem for the missionary as it is in so many countries, even today. In Cambodia's cities, the literacy rate is over 85 percent; and even in the rural areas, at least 60 percent are literate.

A temple inscription in Angkor gives a clue to this widespread emphasis:

> Having drunk the nectar of knowledge,
> the king gave it to others to drink.

With this brief overview of the Khmer people, we will move on to what God is doing in their midst.

3

The Idol-Maker's Son

I felt a kind of excitement building up inside as the car approached our destination. In the company of the Reverend Grady Mangham, I was about to meet the very first Protestant missionaries to Cambodia. They had half a century of living in Cambodia to contribute! A tall, spare-frame man; a brisk cheerful woman, they graciously welcomed us into their sunny living room on a crisp spring day in New York State.

It took little nudging for them to reminisce about their experiences half a world away.

"What does it do to you," I inquired, "when you hear of the great turning to Christ in Cambodia these days?"

With a world of longing in her voice and in her eyes, Mrs. Hammond replied, "Oh, what I would give to be back there!"

We discussed possible explanations of the upsurge

of spiritual interest, and a new one surfaced (new in that no one had pinpointed it as a major factor). Perhaps because it had been one of her special ministries, Mrs. Hammond was the one who mentioned it.

"It was the children's meetings," she told me. "These young people who are accepting the Lord now had grown up, many of them, knowing Bible verses and singing hymns and choruses. We always had children's meetings. We had four hundred memorizing Scripture; many university students had been brought up in childrens' meetings."

Listening to this spritely retired missionary, I was reminded of the frequent mention of children's work in the historical records made available to me by the Alliance.

What was true about children and young people's work in the '20s with the pioneer missionaries is equally true in the 1960s with those who followed. And success in winning adults was still minimal.

Of their earlier days in Cambodia, Norman and Marie Ens remember, "Only a few adults had accepted the Lord." It was a sadness to them that no church was formed on their station in the provinces at that time. Their ministry was mostly among children and young people who as they grew older left for the city of Phnom Penh, and the missionaries lost track of them. When in 1964 the American missionaries had to leave Cambodia, some of the young people seemed to become disillusioned.

"I want to tell you about one of these young fellows," says Mr. Ens, "Leang Long, a fifteen-year-old at that time. He accepted the Lord, and he got himself a great big Bible (at that time the only Bible in Cambodian was this big size). He was short for his age, and that Bible must have been quite

a weight for him to carry around. But Leang loved
that Bible and was one of our staunchest young
believers. But when he took his Bible home, his
father was very angry with him and took the Bible
away from him, burned it, then severely beat his son
for accepting a foreigner's religion. Well, after we had
to leave, Leang Long didn't know where to have
Christian fellowship, and finally he just kind of drifted
away from the things of the Lord. I often thought
about him; when I showed my slides while on
furlough, there was Leang Long in his striped T-shirt,
hugging his big Bible, a broad smile on his face. I
would wonder where he was, and pray for him. I lost
track of him completely and didn't know where to
look for him when we were able to return to
Cambodia.

"Then, after ten years, all of a sudden, Leang Long
(he's now married and has a little baby) came to the
Bethany Bookstore in Phnom Penh. As I heard it, he
just looked around and saw an *Alliance Witness*. I had
given all my copies of the magazine to the store, and
Leang Long noticed my name on the one he picked
up. He immediately quizzed the man in charge,
asking, 'Is he still here? Is Mr. Ens still here?' The
man said 'Yes, he lives near the market' and he gave
Leang my address.

"He was beaming when he came and said, 'Do you
know me?' I said, 'No, I don't think so.'

" 'Well,' he grinned as he started to explain, 'I am
Leang Long from—' but that grin did it. I saw him
just as he used to be! He was now a schoolteacher
and he said, 'It's now ten years and I really want to
come back to the Lord and follow him all my life, and
I want my wife to follow him too.'

"It was like a *miracle*! After all our prayers, God
had brought him back to us. My wife and I agreed to

meet him and his wife in church the following morning, and the very man who had talked with him in the bookstore was preaching. As we were sitting together, Leang Long and I, we were just enjoying the message so much; it was hitting right at his heart and he was nudging me all the time, saying, 'Isn't that *good?*' Then as soon as the service was over, he wanted to get right with the Lord. He did ask a few questions. One that bothered him was this:

" 'Since God is the Creator and made man, why would he make such a man as could turn against him? That just doesn't work. A carpenter makes a chair for his own comfort, not one with prongs sticking out somewhere that are going to jab him. Nor will a man build a car that is going to all of a sudden blow up in his face. Yet here is God—an all-wise God—and he makes a man that can turn on him! And when you talk about the fact that—well, he gives a man free choice—that just doesn't add up. I still can't figure out why God would make a man like that.' "

Obviously the Lord was right there, not one bit disturbed by Leang Long's questionings. And the Holy Spirit must have given special wisdom to the young preacher who was trying to answer his questions. The preacher latched on to the illustration of the car and reasoned with him, "If that car is made for gasoline and you put diesel oil in it, that's not going to work."

Leang Long just pondered that for a minute before replying, "Oh, so God had some laws for man to follow."

"Yes," the preacher agreed, "and man disobeyed."

Now the whole thing was clear to Leang Long.

Norm Ens says, "I couldn't help thanking the Lord for giving real wisdom to the preacher to answer as he

did. That was the very last Sunday we were in
Cambodia. So my wife and I felt the Lord was
ministering to us too, assuring us that he can be with
the Christians, can give them the right message, can
give Cambodian spiritual leaders the answers to
people's questions. It was as though the Lord was
telling us not to worry but to leave our beloved
Cambodians to him."

The young man, Leang Long, amply bears out Mrs.
Hammond's thesis about the worth of children's and
youth work.

Another example is a man whom God has used
effectively since he forsook Buddhism to follow the
living Christ. This man's background and his father's
vocation were not such as one would expect to
produce the climate for conversion to Christianity.
From Manila Mr. Lim Chheong shares his own story:

I was born into a Buddhist family. My father was an
idol-maker. From silver and gold he formed statues of
Buddha and sold them for a great deal of money. He
also made some for us to worship as a family.

I was ten years old when my uncle, who was a
Buddhist monk, taught me the Buddhist doctrines.
He told me that Buddha was born higher than man,
that he lived a life that was higher than any man. My
uncle tried to live a perfect life every day so that he
could go to heaven.

When I was fifteen years old, I began to ask
questions and tried to search further about going to
heaven. I asked my uncle about the problem of sin:
How can I get out from doing bad, from sinning?
"Nobody can get out from doing bad things;
everyone has sinned," he answered. "But if you will
try hard to live according to the teaching of Buddha,
you will become perfect." He also said, "Don't kill

anything that has life. If you kill anything—like the animal or the insect, even mosquitoes, ants, and flies—you will go to hell." I said to my uncle, "I don't have any hope any more to go to heaven because already I've killed many things that have life."

I felt sad and frustrated because Buddha could not help me. To myself I was saying, "I cannot fulfill all the 'don'ts' of Buddha's teaching." But God saw the desire of my heart. He knew that I was searching for the real meaning of life. He sent ministers to help me.

One Sunday morning I heard the children from our neighbor's house singing a song about Jesus Christ. I was curious about what they were doing and I went to listen. After telling the story, the teacher handed out beautiful Christmas cards. I liked it. From that time on I began to attend and listen carefully to the stories and the songs. They were always happy.

I wanted to be happy. I wanted to know more about this Jesus.

The teacher saw my interest; she told me about Jesus who died on the Cross for my sin.

"Jesus can get the sin away from the heart of people," she told me. "He lives again to give life to all who receive him."

Then I began to ask many questions, and the teacher was able to answer them from the Bible. And she explained very clearly about God. At this time I accepted Christ as my personal Savior. That was in 1953, in Kampong Cham province. I was then 15 years old.

My life has changed. I love to hear more about Jesus Christ. I am very happy to go to church every time. I have joy in my heart.

My father learned about my decision, so he tried to

stop me from believing in Jesus Christ. He
threatened me and made me stop going to church.
One night I came from the church at nine o'clock,
and when I reached home, my father got angry with
me. Then I went to sleep. At about eleven o'clock he
called me out from the room and put me outside the
house and closed the door. He said, "You are not my
son any more. Get out from this house and go sleep
with your God!" From that time I started to pray and
asked the Lord to help me, to give me a place to
sleep and live. God answered my prayer. He sent my
brother-in-law, who took me to his house. That was
the time when I learned to pray, to ask God, and I
learned to trust the Lord.

God calls me to the ministry
In the year 1959, I finished the public school, then
went to work for the government. My father was now
very happy because I had a job and the pride of
working with the government. Then one night as I
read my Bible, the Lord called me to go to Bible
school and study to serve him.

> "The harvest is so great, and the workers are so
> few . . . So pray to the one in charge of the
> harvesting, and ask him to recruit more workers
> for his harvest fields" (Matthew 9:37, 38).
> "Also I heard the voice of the Lord, saying,
> Whom shall I send, and who will go for us?
> Then said I, Here am I; send me" (Isaiah 6:8).

But I didn't want to become a pastor, because a
pastor is a poor man; no salary. So I said to the Lord,
"Lord, let me work with the government and I can go
to church and help the pastor with my salary. I think
I can help in the church and that will be very good."
But God continued speaking to me about the

ministry. Then one night I had a very high fever. I
thought I would die, and I cried to the Lord for help,
to heal me. I promised that by the next day, I would
go to Bible school. And the Lord very quickly
answered my prayer.

In the morning when I woke up I was very fine, so
I went to Bible school. First I told my mother about
my decision. She cried and told my father that I
would leave my work and go to Bible school. My
father got mad at me and angrily shouted, "If you go
to Bible school, I will not consider you any more my
son. You are not my son any more!"

The Lord reminded me of the promise I made that
evening, so I said, "I'd rather obey God and go to
Bible school because he is calling me."

The Bible school was 134 kilometers away from our
home. I didn't have a single cent. How could I go? I
prayed and asked the Lord for money (now that I
could truly say, "Here am I; send me"). I told the
pastor of my church about my decision, and the
church gave me money enough for me to get to the
Bible school and to pay for the first semester. Some
of my brothers and sisters in Christ sent money to
help me so that I had more than I needed. Praise the
Lord! So I was able to study at Takhman Bible
Institute for four years and the Lord faithfully
provided my needs, even though my parents never
sent money and never answered my letters.

I'll never forget the most wonderful experience
when, in April 1963, I graduated. As the choir sang
and the organ played, I marched toward the altar as if
I were walking toward heaven. The commission that
was given by the minister, Rev. Merle Graven, was a
direct word from God, speaking to me. So I said to
the Lord, "Lord, I will go where you want me to go,
and I will do what you want me to do."

My mother comes to the Lord
In my third year in Bible school, my mother came
and visited for three days with me. She came because
she loves me and she missed me very much. So,
praise the Lord, I had this opportunity to speak to her
about how Jesus saved me from sin. He changed my
life. He loves me and he loves her too. She
understood what I meant because she loves me, but
she did not accept Jesus Christ right away; she was
afraid of my father.

In my fourth year at Bible school, during the
Christmas break, I received a telegram telling me my
mother was seriously ill at the hospital. Before going
home, I met the Lord first, asking him to show his
miracle in the life of my mother at her bedside. I
stood looking at her face and praying that God
through his Holy Spirit would open the way for me to
witness to my mother again.

After a short greeting, I talked to her again about
the saving knowledge of the Lord Jesus Christ. I saw
her very weak, so I told her, "The one thing I can do
for you is show you that Jesus alone can help you.
You need to accept him as your personal Savior. He
is the one who can save you from sin and he can heal
you from your sickness." She answered me, "My sin
is really great, and I truly need him to save me
because Buddha cannot save me. When I die, I am
sure I will go to hell. But I am afraid that when your
father knows that I have accepted Jesus, he will get
angry with me or with you, my son."

"Do you want to please my father and die and go
to hell," I asked her, "or do you want to be saved
from your sin and go to heaven and my father will get
angry with you? Which way will you choose?"

Mother's reply was to ask me to call my father
because she wanted to ask him some questions. I

went and called my father and when he came, my
mother said to him, "Now I know I cannot live
longer any more, and my sin is very heavy. I need
Jesus. I want to accept him as Lim Chheong our son
has done."

"It's up to you," my father said and he went out of
the room.

"You see!" I told my mother. "Father said it's up
to you. So you are the one to decide for yourself."

She said, "How can I accept Jesus?"

So I explained, "You pray with me and I will lead
you to confess your sin and receive Jesus to come
into your heart as your Savior and Lord." She agreed
and I was so glad that I could lead my mother to the
Lord.

Through the goodness of the Lord my mother got
well (although the doctor told me that she had been
just waiting for her death that day). But, praise God,
for six months she was well; she could go to the
market every day, cook food, and wash clothes. Then
after my graduation, I again received a telegram,
saying my mother had passed away. I was comforted
and had peace in my heart because my mother came
to the Lord.

Opening for further study
During my senior year, there was a desire in my heart
for further study. I wanted to learn more about God's
Word and other subject matter, to be well prepared
for the ministry. So I told the Lord about it. And four
months before my graduation, I received word that
the Lord had provided for me to go abroad to study
so I could see his work in other countries. God
opened the way for me to go to the Philippines to
study at Ebenezer Bible College. Oh, how I rejoice

and praise the Lord. This year is really hard for me to study the Bible in English. In my country we used our own Cambodian, so my English was very poor.

I planned to study four or five years in the Philippines, but after eight months of struggles at Ebenezer, I received news from my country asking me to go back home. The relationship between the United States and my country was cut off; all the missionaries must go back to their own homeland and I have to fill up the work that they have left.

When all missionaries left Cambodia in 1965, the governor required all pastors and workers to sign a paper declaring that we would promise to close the door of the church and stop preaching the Word of God. This was a severe trial for all of us. We were all brought before police officers, then they told us we had to sign the paper.

There were four of us pastors and workers in the church. They put us in prison and threatened constantly that they would kill us because we continued to work for the Lord. *I could not sign the paper.* I said, "I will not close the door of the church and will keep on preaching the gospel forever, for Jesus told me to do this." It made the authorities more and more angry.

Inside the prison cell, four of us gathered together every day to pray and sing and read God's Word (my wife had, after much trying, succeeded in getting Bibles to us in the prison). Like Paul did in his prison cell, we began to preach, and God rewarded us for our faithfulness to him with twelve souls, and others were able to listen to his Word.

With the twelve converts we began our Sunday service. We were in prison for two and a half months; during this time, my faithful wife continued to send food and other things we asked her to send. This was done secretly through someone we trusted.

[Another brave pastor, imprisoned on a different occasion, is Fifi, a Chinese man credited with winning many souls. He is fluent in Cambodian, Chinese, and Vietnamese. The missionaries tell of receiving a telegram from the provinces saying, "Fifi is in jail; please pray" (this was one of four imprisonments he had undergone for preaching the gospel). The missionaries did pray; they knew how to pray for Fifi, and they praised God. A few days later, word came that Fifi had been released: "They couldn't stand him!"

A moving incident came out of the imprisonment of the four pastors. Major Chhirc, not permitted to visit the Christians, took up his position outside the jail so that his brethren inside could see him and take comfort—Author.]

From 1964 to 1970, the work of the Lord in Cambodia was hard; there were great trials and testings. Those were days when we had to stand for the Lord, and through his grace and the strength he gave us, we were able to go through it. Praise the Lord, for in those years of hardship he provided for us a missionary couple from France, Rev. and Mrs. Jean Fune, who encouraged us and helped us to continue the work. (While U. S. visas were not being granted, this French couple were able to reenter Cambodia at that time.)

The door reopens

God had his purpose in closing Cambodia. He saw that there are still people who will open their hearts to his Word if only there are those who faithfully and diligently work for him.

In 1970, the Lord reopened the work in Cambodia *wide*. Missionaries—American, Swiss, British, and

Canadian—were permitted to enter again. This time
they worked harder than ever, taking every
opportunity to interest the people. Many came to the
Lord and the church grew very fast—from two to
twenty-eight groups, with about 10,000 believers. As
workers for the Lord, we must take every
opportunity. As Paul wrote, we must "redeem the
time" as if each one is our very last opportunity to
witness. Not only must we take them; we must *make*
opportunities to witness, for each one might indeed
be the last and the door could be closed again.

I praise the Lord that at this time, my father
stopped making Buddha idols. He started to come to
church and I was privileged to bring some of my
sisters and brothers to accept the Lord as their Savior.

New home, new ministry
The closing of the door of Cambodia in 1964 was a
closing door also for my furthering my study at
Ebenezer. The opening of that door was likewise a
reopening of the door of study. In 1974 God gave me
the privilege of renewing my studies at Ebenezer.
And the scholarship provided for my whole family.

The trouble in Cambodia was getting serious. It
seemed just impossible for us to get necessary
documents to go out of the country, but we prayed
and trusted the Lord to do this for us if it was his
will. And God did help us; in just three days the
papers were prepared and signed by the government
officials.

On May 28, 1974, we reached our new home at
Ebenezer Bible College, Zamboanga City,
Philippines. My prayer was that as I trusted the Lord,
he would enable me to finish my Bachelor of
Ministerial Studies. I hoped to eventually teach and

administer the Takhman Bible Institute in Cambodia.

It was a hard struggle again. Back to school after a number of years, and again, the English language which I had not studied in public school, so it was a problem to me in my studies. I cannot understand it and speak it well. But through God's help and the wisdom he gave me, I graduated on March 9, 1975. *Now*, I thought, *I can go back to my country and serve God.* But a few weeks after my graduation, my heart grieved and with my family I cried, because of the fall of my country to the enemy. The question on my heart was, Will I see and meet my people in Cambodia again, is this possible?

God knows my heart. He knew that personal evangelism was closed to me—taking the gospel to my people, helping them to see that Jesus Christ is the answer to life's question. Yet, in his all-knowing wisdom, God chose another means for me; he opened another door for my family and me to serve our own people in Cambodia. He provided us with a radio ministry working with the Far East Broadcasting Company in Manila. The Lord also provided us with another wonderful experience. We arrived in Manila and had to apply for a passport to remain another year in the Philippines. Later, we learned that the Cambodia embassy was closed right after they signed our passport! Our God is always on time to meet important matters.

With another Cambodian broadcaster, Keam Nuy, my wife and I broadcast the Word of God to the Cambodians. When the other method of reaching the people is closed, God opens up another way for witnessing to them. At present we are working hard each day, translating and typing programs to reach our own people with the gospel message in their own language.

Our hearts cry for Cambodia, remembering the
great trials and persecutions the Christians—some of
them my own relatives—are suffering right now. Will
you please pray for strength and courage and boldness
for them to stand for the Lord. May they remain
faithful even if it means death for them! And pray for
the Cambodia radio program that through it, many of
my people will come to know Christ as their personal
Lord and Savior.

We are very grateful and thankful to God for all
who help and pray for us. Praise the Lord!

What of the fellow broadcaster to whom Lim
Chheong made reference, Keam Nuy?

We'll let her introduce herself:

Approximately seven million people live in my
country today. Most of them are Buddhists. For a
long time Christians were not allowed to do
evangelistic work in Cambodia. Hence my people
have lived in darkness not knowing that Christ, the
light of the world, came to bring light to their
darkened souls. That's why I'm so thrilled to be here
at FEBC (Far East Broadcasting Company) to present
Jesus Christ to my own people through the magic of
radio.

Sad to say, I have not always felt this way about
Jesus Christ nor about serving him. In fact, there was
a time when I hated my parents because they served
the Lord. My father is a pastor of the National
Evangelical Church in Cambodia, and I was raised in a
Christian home. During my early childhood, I
believed everything my parents told me about Jesus
Christ. However, when I was thirteen, I went to the
city to study. There I lived with a family of
unbelievers. They knew I came from a Christian

family, and they wanted to break me from my Christianity. Many times they told me, "If we do good, we become good; if we do bad, we become bad."

Believing this to be the truth, I tried to follow their teaching by doing good and trying to please all my friends. I enjoyed living with my foster family. They took care of all my needs. I was also very happy with my friends. My parents I learned to hate, because I thought my friends were better than they. My parents always called me to pray and read the Bible. I didn't like that. I didn't like them to be serving the Lord either.

My parents soon observed my attitude; they saw that I was drifting away, and they began to pray for me. One day I saw my father praying with tears in his eyes. I was worried, but something in my mind said, "Well, he is a pastor: he has to pray for the Christians and for the family. I should not worry about that." I forced myself to forget my parents.

But because my parents really loved the Lord, they wanted to see my life changed. So they sent me to Bible school. The first year in that school was miserable for me. I kept writing my parents begging them to take me back home, because I wanted to be a teacher in the government service. (I'm glad now that my parents did not heed my requests!)

In my second year, a pastor from Indonesia spoke in chapel about being born again. The Holy Spirit spoke to my heart and made me realize my need. I confessed to Jesus Christ that I was a sinner, and received him as Lord and Savior. Since that time, I have learned to love Jesus Christ, and he has taught me to love my parents.

After Bible school, I worked with the National Evangelical Church. Then in August 1973, the Lord

called me to serve him in South Viet Nam. It was there I met the Filipino missionary who was to be my husband. He shared the same commitment that I have to serve the Lord. After our engagement, God called me to work for him as a broadcaster at the Far East Broadcasting Company here in Manila.

I am so happy for God's leading in our lives. I thank him for this opportunity to work for him among my own people. God uses anyone who is willing to be used of him. He can use you, too, if you will give yourself to him.

Keam's testimony could be that of any young person brought up in a Christian home with godly, concerned parents. And, as happens both in the East and the West, our long-suffering God can wait for the return of the rebel in answer to the fervent prayer of the parents.

It's particularly thrilling to share this happy ending in the light of something I read in the *Evangelical Press News Service,* dated June 14, 1975:*

> Two pastors who escaped from Da Nang and Nha Trang in the early days of Communist advancement . . . said the Reds allowed the people under their control to listen to only one radio station—missionary broadcasts sponsored by the Far East Broadcasting Company.
>
> "Everybody was listening to FEBC," said Mrs. Bich Quang, FEBC's director in Saigon, before her evacuation. "This sounds strange to us, but

*Author's note: Later, Dr. Le Hoang Phu modified this statement. He said that it was not that the Reds named FEBC as the one station which the people could listen to; rather, they forbade them to listen to a list of radio stations that were indicated as not acceptable. They did not list FEBC; therefore, it was interpreted that the Reds would permit the people to listen to that particular station. Mr. Mangham has confirmed this.

it might be the Lord who does this to give us the greatest opportunity in Viet Nam that we have ever had.''

True, that's Viet Nam, not Cambodia. We rejoice for Viet Nam, and since the same mentality undoubtedly governs the Communists in Cambodia, we can pray that the same opportunity is being afforded the controlled people there.

For her part, Keam Nuy is there in Manila, ready and able to broadcast to her own people in their own tongue.

And right in there with her is the son of the idol-maker, Lim Chheong and his wife.

4

Wheelchairs, Noah's Ark, and a Warehouse

Some stories are so engrossing that everybody wants to tell them. Such was the tale of the amputees' church. It became almost routine as I interviewed missionary after missionary evacuated from Phnom Penh to have them say, "I'm sure you've already heard about the amputees' church," or as some called it, "the wheelchair church," or "the church in Andy Bishop's house." They were right. I had heard. But I listened again, for they were eager to tell it and it was none the less inspiring each time it was told.

Again, as is true in so much of the outreach that produced impressive results, national Christians initiated the witness among the hospitalized amputees and paraplegics. Five years of war had created a heavy patient load. This was aggravated by the shortage of crutches and wheelchairs that decreed these must be left behind when the patient left. Can you imagine the patient's dilemma? Some, therefore, opted to remain rather than face life on the outside without the necessary aids. But they were not "forgotten men" (as are some veterans). Two young Cambodian fellows who had been Christians for about a year got a real burden for the men in the hospital and proceeded to do something about it.

"The hospital was quite near our home," Norman Ens explained, "so the two came and stocked up on literature and began to visit the men, and it was no more than two or three weeks until forty of the patients accepted the Lord. Next, the concerned fellows began to think of ways of getting the new believers to a worship service. But where, and how would they get there?"

But before long, difficulty of transportation and the discomfort of the patients pointed out the impracticality of taking them a long distance to an evangelical church week after week. Then one day, Mr. Amkhit, who was one of those who had witnessed to the amputees, went to Mr. Andrew Bishop, administrator of the new hospital in Phnom Penh, and shared his burden for this group of new Christians. They needed their own place to meet, he explained. And Andy had a solution to this problem.

"Would they like to come to my home?" he asked. "We have room for forty people, and we'd be glad to host a church in our house. That's no problem."

The offer was readily accepted. Missionaries and medical personnel dug into their pockets for the mini-bus fares to take the men and their wheelchairs for the shorter ride to Andy Bishop's house. Thirty-five came that first Sunday.

Young Dr. Charles Folkstad added his enthusiastic report of that service and its aftermath: "It was supposed to start at 9:30," he said, "and I arrived on

time to find them already singing heartily. Andy told me, 'I got out of bed at 7:30 and the fellows were here already.' The yard has a large cement area where the wheelchairs were set up but even with their wheelchairs, the first service was so long the men could hardly stand it. Then the two Cambodian Christians who had initiated the whole thing realized the problem. *They* were doing the preaching. Wisely they concluded, 'We love the Lord and we love these amputee guys, but we just don't know enough to preach.' They were smart enough to realize that (and they'd been smart enough to witness and to win the men to Christ in that hospital).

"Andy had been able to get a bunch of crutches from a disaster hospital. So after the preaching, we began to fit some of the guys with crutches. The smiles on their faces—the thankfulness—was just unbelievable. It was one of the most touching services I've ever been in. I'll never, never forget those guys."

I should say that Chuck Folkstad would be good for people even if he were not a doctor. Looking like an American All-Star football player, he and his buddy, Mr. Bob Beck, had six months between medical school and residency and decided to serve the Lord in the C & MA medical program (later they worked also with World Vision) in Cambodia. There's a warmth, a compassion that oozes from 6'6" Chuck Folkstad from Minnesota.

A member of the Overseas Missionary Fellowship (OMF), Don Cormack, shared his impressions of the crippled soldiers before and after their exposure to the gospel and Christian compassion in action:

"Battered, broken men huddled two or three to a bed. The ravages of war had made the medical situation impossible. The glazed eyes of the amputees, with no hope left in them, met mine and my heart ached for them."

With some young Khmer Christians, Don shared the message of Easter, that in Jesus there is something to live for *today*, and for the future—the glad assurance of eternal life with Christ.

Many for whom life had been a living death responded to the message. Men who had lain listless for weeks became *people*, people with a determination to live again. They were no longer content to live like animals. These patients began to help in the wards; they started to clean up and remove the filth; they were able in a number of little ways to help the nurses and doctors whose task was almost beyond human resources.

And as always when Christian conversion results in positive, demonstrated change, the non-Christian began to take notice. The governor of one of these hospitals said to Don Cormack, "I don't know much about Christianity, but if it can transform my men like this, I want to know all I can about it."[1]

"Some of the fellows had not been able to learn to walk since the amputation, because they'd had no crutches. So it was a thrill for us as well as for them," says Andy Bishop, "to fit them and then show them how to use the crutches."

One of the incidents that's been told and retold just has to be a missionary "first." One of the patients who came to be fitted for crutches following a Sunday morning service appeared to be making out

[1]This item was contributed to me by Dr. Anne Townsend, OMF missionary. Used with permission of OMF.

quite well, hobbling on one good leg and one artificial one. Andy explained, "Crutches will just be a bother to you. You'll get to be dependent on them and you won't learn to use that wooden leg properly." The man wouldn't be discouraged, however. When the men were working on the fittings, the question again arose. Chuck Folkstad recalls, "I was working through an interpreter and I couldn't quite understand why this guy needed crutches. Then he said, 'I don't have an artificial leg; this one's not mine. I just borrowed it from a friend so I could come to church. I have to give it back to him when I get back to the hospital.'"

At the time of this incident, the church had grown to seventy-five or eighty believers. Not only were they meeting on Sundays, but they also had two Bible studies a week, and once a week they met for prayer at Andy's house. Not content with that, some of the veteran amputees were out on the streets witnessing and selling Christian literature. By this means, others—not handicapped persons—were becoming a part of this church group. Nor did this growth cease with the forced pullout of the missionaries. Subsequently, Gene Hall was permitted to return for about two weeks and what did he find?

"What a sight as I had the privilege of speaking on Easter Sunday at the amputees' church; no pews; no benches; all wheelchairs except for some seated on the cement—and one hundred and six present!"

It was there that Sunday morning that the leader of the group pleaded, "I've got to have lessons to teach these people." This man wasn't thinking about war, about the enemy approaching the city.

As Norman Ens raved about this particular group in Phnom Penh, he added an item from a letter he had received after he was evacuated. The letter was written by the man to whom he had turned over the literature responsibility and who had also been left in charge of Andy Bishop's house. There he had been holding three Bible studies a week. He just taught the others what he himself had been taught in Bible school, and thirty-five new believers had been added at the time he wrote this letter to Mr. Ens.

"One of the subjects I taught in Bible school," Norman told me, "was church history and I feel this was exactly right preparation for the people at that time."

The lessons of history, the awareness of the courage and endurance of Christians through the centuries—this input might well account for what a *Time* magazine correspondent observed as "an expectation of persecution and willingness to face it." Certain it is that some Cambodian believers voiced this expectation and more than one declared, "If I have to die, I want the last thing I do to be telling about Jesus, the living Christ."

This, then, is The Church of the Amputees, the Wheelchair Church, the Church in Andy Bishop's House—the name doesn't matter. Actually, the church of Jesus Christ is wherever a group of believers gather in his name.

The Khmer Christians have not allowed the lack of physical, ecclesiastical facilities to cramp them. As both Tom Wisley and Gene Hall reminded me, "These people have not studied the principles of church growth; they have not been privileged to attend Dr. McGavran's School of World Mission." Nevertheless, church growth is a phenomenon of the '70s in the Khmer Republic. Michael Green's comment at Lausanne, "The early church did not have a strategy," might well apply to the Khmer church.

Another of the churches has the intriguing name
"Noah's Ark Church." Like the amputees' church,
this too grew out of necessity. One Sunday Mr. Thay
Thong went to church and found it so crowded that
some people had no place to sit down. "This should
not be," he determined. Himself a believer of just six
months, he was concerned that other places of
worship should be started, to accommodate those who
wanted to hear the gospel. With the attitude that
seems to characterize these gospel-aroused
Cambodians, he went into action.

God laid it on his heart to use an old boat he had
dry-docked out in the middle of a field. Its ancient
appearance lent itself well to the name "Noah's
Ark." People learned about this new "church," and
thirty adults and 200 children came to the first service
held there. Field chairman Hall met with the elders of
this church and found them "extremely capable" and
laying plans for evangelizing and teaching.

Speaking of such new churches, Gene Hall
comments, "The material assets of the Khmer Church
are meagre, but there's a fresh richness, a vibrancy in
their newfound faith. The growth in the church has
far outpaced the church buildings; for this reason the
term 'church groups' is used. They're poverty level in
buildings, but rich in the Spirit!"

Some of the stories of church beginnings and
church growth vibrate with Book of Acts fervency
and excitement. Take the Tuol Kok Dike Church as
an example: Mr. Son Sonne was discipling a group of
young men at his house. He encouraged them to start
a Bible study in their homes and so Son Hour
volunteered. Son Sonne arrived, and to his
amazement found about 100 persons present. At the
close 71 accepted Christ. The next day they had
another "Bible Study" with 300 attending and 200

turning to Christ. Each successive meeting saw others respond until around 1600 met Christ. Their meeting place, their church? An abandoned warehouse! So this had become "The Warehouse Church."

The Wheelchair Church. Noah's Ark Church. The Warehouse Church. What matters the building or the circumstances? The church of Jesus Christ has met behind closed doors, in caves, in catacombs, in prisons, on the open meadows, on the high seas.

As one new Christian in Cambodia expressed it, "The greatest thing is not your church. It's your Jesus."

But Who Is the Monkey's Ancestor?

Students and school teachers are notable among the enthusiasts in Cambodia's spiritual revolution.

What are the teachings they've grappled with, the bred-in-the-bone tenets of Buddhism that can never coexist with the teachings of Jesus? Creation, for instance. Buddhism views this world as having four distinct elements—earth, water, fire, and wind—linked together by primary and secondary causes without any plan or purpose, and certainly not created by God. Add to this the Buddhist's traditional belief in cause and effect in a series of reincarnations. Set this against "In the beginning God created the heavens and the earth . . . and God said, Let us make man in our image . . ."

To my surprise a one-time missionary to Cambodia said to me, "I'm hearing about all the conversions over there. But don't take that too seriously. I know the Cambodians; they'll never stand. Most of the so-called converts will give up.''

This was neither sour grapes nor the opinion of a negative person. It was an assessment based on long years of experience with the Khmer people. He didn't have the joy of seeing scores, hundreds come to Christ in Cambodia, nor the ''sadness'' of many converts with but few to shepherd them! What he was saying was, *"Buddhists do not change.* They may profess to do so, but once a Buddhist, always a Buddhist.''

Nevertheless this thinking is knocked into a cocked hat as new Christians in Cambodia beautifully express their belief and how it came about.

A Canadian, Miss Ruth Patterson, generously shared with me some treasured letters from students with whom she had worked.

An RN, Ruth had served on the medical team in the C & MA's Zaire (then Congo) field. But statistics in the mission's prayer manual disturbed her, especially the pitiable ratio of Christians in Cambodia with those in Congo. She found herself in tears at times, as she prayed for Cambodia. As a hospital was proposed for Phnom Penh, circumstances combined to make it possible for Ruth to be assigned there. The African Christians beautifully accepted her going when she suggested she could be *their missionary* to the Khmer people.

The strong feeling that Cambodia was God's place for her at that time was soon vindicated for Ruth Patterson.

''I've never known anything like it in my life,'' she relates. ''It was actually true that Buddhist priests and others came knocking at our door, and as we opened it they would say, 'Please tell me about Jesus.' One Buddhist priest said to me, 'Tell me *all about him*—I want to know all about him, right from the

beginning.' Never have I seen such beautiful openness and such hunger for the gospel in the lives of people.''

She had been in the city of Phnom Penh just a few days when a Buddhist monk, setting aside all cultural and religious mores which would have forbade such behavior, approached her and asked her where she lived. He then came bringing another monk with him, and later they brought some students. This led to classes being held in English and in Bible, and many made decisions to follow Christ as a result. I might add here that this heart hunger of Buddhist monks was not unknown some years ago. A friend of mine taught English to members of the royal family in the palace in Phnom Penh. He even taught Lon Nol, later the ruling figure of Cambodia. This man, Richard Miller, now head librarian in Arcadia, California, has told me about his contacts with Buddhist monks. One asked him if he might come alone to visit and when he did, without any preamble he stated, "I've come to have you tell me how I can receive Jesus as my Savior.''

And what of Miss Rose Ellen Chancey, OMF missionary? "I had been in Phnom Penh just one hour," she said, "when I found myself leading a Bible study in English, and teaching Bible-hungry Khmer young people. I couldn't believe it!''

Because the hospital was still in the building stages, Ruth, working with Norm Ens, head of the literature department, took over the English-speaking correspondence school responsibilities.

Using the Gospel of John (TEV), which is especially good with Asians, the courses covered the beginnings: one God—Christ, the Son of God—the problems of life. "This all leads to a very good understanding of the Scriptures,'' says Miss Patterson.

The method of teaching was simple explanation and questions to be answered by the student. One section asked for a personal decision: Have *you* received Jesus? When? Where?

Some people have said that all the spiritual activity has been among the refugees in Cambodia. Here, as we peek over Ruth Patterson's shoulder as she reads the responses from a cross section of correspondence school students, we will meet people from various walks of life. About 250 were enrolled in the courses, and here are some gems from their letters.

A HIGH SCHOOL STUDENT IN BATTAMBANG:
Up to this date the English language and the Christ religion are the most important thing in our world. Knowing this, I everyday try to learn English hard, and look for some doctrine about Jesus. But I receive only the insufficient result: Both are very scarce in my country. Sometimes I despair because I cannot realize my purpose, but when I feel like this, one idea always consoles me. It is this, that if I try, one day my dream will be real. So, one year ago, I try by all means. Luckily one of my friends told me that there is a company that broadcasts a radio program and they always give the address of that company. Now I know my friend's news is true. I am very fond of that program and on Saturdays and Sundays I am usually near the radio looking for these programs.

But I have no documents to follow it. So I don't understand and after the program is ended, its meaning sound seems to dry up from my mind. So I ask you, please, for some documents to follow your program in purpose to diffuse the Christ religion about Jesus all over the world.

(Second letter from the same student)

. . . received your letter with a copy of Good
News told by John, and five lessons and some
informations. Intentions to study the course
because it can make me close to God and his
speeches. I am studying on my own. I read the
questions one by one, carefully, and try to find
exact meaning so I can answer well. But,
however, some questions I don't understand
very well, so the answer is not clear. Too, I beg
your pardon that the writing is not always clear
because my ballpoint pen is not well. I hope you
will try to make understanding yourself.

A SCHOOLTEACHER IN SIEM REAP:
I feel extremely excited when writing this short
letter. I ought to tell you that great excitement
always occurs in me when I write, or think, or
talk about God—the true God that can save me
out of Satan's power and can give me a life
beyond the grave.

But what is in me is still doubtful and dull, for
I know God very little. Frankly speaking, I am in
search of a way that can make me very happy (as
are many other people of our world).

How to lead a clean life? It's a question I
always ask myself. I know perfectly that I am a
sinner. I am longing to have peace in my mind.
So is it not that I need a Savior?

Now let me tell you something. I am now
studying the Bible course with great interest,
reading the lessons, answering the questions.
The questions are my true pleasure . . . I am
ambitious to know more about God, Christ, and
the Christian religion. I have to tell you that I

now possess a New Testament! It's a gift from the Evangelical Church.

I suppose you know I was born not a Christian. I want to turn to the true God. I don't want to be a lost sheep any more.

Rev. Norman Ens went to this city to meet with correspondence students and some Christians living there, and a church group was formed. The missionary contacted the schoolteacher who wrote this letter and talked with him. Asked, "Are you a Christian?" the teacher replied, "You see, I don't know because I haven't had anybody to teach me like the Ethiopian eunuch and to explain to me clearly."

So Ens "explained and showed him clearly" that in order to become a Christian, he must believe in Jesus and receive him as his personal Savior.

"Then I'm a Christian!" exclaimed the schoolteacher. "That's what I did. I believed in Jesus and I received him into my heart." God blessed that man and his witness. He was given the opportunity to go to New Zealand for study and he is there now.

A COMMUNITY DEVELOPMENT WORKER
IN SIEM REAP:
Since December (when work was begun in that city) I am a Christian. I have found the words of God that they are very true. I hope you will send a teacher for leading the Christians in Siem Reap. I am reading a Bible from day to day.

ANOTHER SCHOOLTEACHER IN SIEM REAP:
When I finish the Bible correspondence test, I admire them very much. Now I know well about Jesus Christ. I left all my mistakes that I have before. I read the *Good News by a Man Named John* for two days. I did all the exercises. I

lived in darkness, not knowing what is the true
way and what is my true God. And I had no god
in my mind, so I did what I wanted, my own
desires. This wrong doing was for over twenty
years, because of my sin. At present I have a
new life because of the Lord. Having made all
things, he loved the world so much that he gave
his only Son . . . I pray God will help so many
in our country that they may believe also.

THE MAN WHO WROTE THE NATIONAL
ANTHEM OF CAMBODIA, A MIDDLE-AGED MAN:
Before studying the correspondence course I was
a simple believer in God. Frankly, I was not sure
that God was able to help me. When I reached
Lesson Six, I knew many wonderful things about
God. I feel very strong in heart because I am so
sure. God loves me and protects me in all
circumstances. I don't fear any more, even
death. Daily I used to smoke two packets of
cigarettes and now, thanks to God, I do not. I
find happiness and joy growing in my heart. I
can say now because of the Lord God, I have
hope, help, and a good life.

A SCHOOLTEACHER:
Through the correspondence course I have
learned many things. I knew who is the true God
who made the world and everything in it. Later
by transgression and disobeying of God, sin
came into the world. God sent his Son into the
world and he died on the cross. Also I received
help in finding the way to a good life. All must
be born again spiritually [this is an especially
meaningful tenet to the reincarnation-oriented
Buddhist—Author], to turn away from his sin

and accept Jesus as his Savior. Whoever takes Jesus into the life to guide all activity, and accepts him as Savior, has a serenity in life, free from judgment.

OFFICER OF POLITICAL WARFARE:
Before, I did what I wanted to do myself. Now after studying these courses, I've noticed some verses that helped me into the good way. I am an ignorant man, but some of these are clear in my mind, helping me to choose the good. Now whatever I do, I always think first of God's Word because its teaching will drive me on in the right way with safety. I've been helped to see a kind way to live and be God's child. I am a military man, but now I am not afraid to go to war. God is with me.

When he came to the section on personal decision, a Buddhist monk wrote:

Question: Do you believe in Jesus as your Savior?
Answer: Yes.
Question: Have you received Jesus?
Answer: Yes, I received Christ when I knew Jesus is the only Son of God.
Question: Where did you receive Jesus Christ?
Answer: At my pagoda residence.

ANOTHER BUDDHIST MONK:
I am a child of God. I know it is quite clear God is the only One. He has made all things in the sky and the earth. Oh, my dear God. Where is God? For I want to see. Please help me. Thank you that you made all people—and me. Thanks, God.

received many good words from Jesus. I liked
this verse very much: "The light is come into
the world . . . you will know the truth and the
truth will set you free."

I want to gather persons to learn the history of
Jesus. But I have no way. I think I have the only
way if I open a class and teach English to them
and I teach the story of Jesus. I don't know very
much myself. But I know that forever I will try
to tell the story of Jesus to my friends.

(A missionary did go and form small groups for Bible
study, after which still another schoolteacher wrote):

Since you left I always think of you and
remember the times we had together. You
taught us God's Word. Since then I grow strong
and I understand God's Word. Yesterday was
Sunday and we met at Mr. H's house. We pray
and we learn God's Word and we have a
wonderful time together.

Every evening before I go to bed, I now pray
to God and I read the Bible. I ask God to help
me to understand his words. I am calm in my
heart and I sleep right away. When I get up I
feel strong. It is wonderful!

A FOURTEEN-YEAR-OLD GIRL:
I began to understand the correspondence
courses and I believed in Jesus when the
missionaries came and taught us.

Yesterday you left Siem Reap, but we are
continuing to teach about Jesus. I have told
people Jesus loves us and forgives us from our
sins and if we believe in him, we will have
eternal life. They all listened to me—and to
God's Son.

(Later this girl writes about her gratitude for the gift of a tape recorder and tapes):

Thank you for your most kind gramophone. I have never received such a wonderful gift! I prayed to God every morning at eight o'clock about this beautiful thing, and now I have received it. I must say, what a wonderful thing that God pitied me; he loves me! I can only say from my heart and from my spirit that I love the Lord. I always speak about Jesus to my fellow students and I play the gramophone for them. So they listen to what God is like, that God loves us, what sin is like, and how God helps us . . . now they want to learn all about Jesus Christ. Also I play the gramophone for my family and my cousins and my friends.

ANOTHER CORRESPONDENCE STUDENT:
. . . I want to learn more about God because I do not know clearly about him, and I think that if you just believe in Jesus and give yourself to him, it is not enough. We must tell the other people as much as we can. So this is what I want to do.

A FEMALE STUDENT:
This Bible course makes clear to me right and wrong—the true God who takes away sin. Now I believe, receive, trust, love, and obey God with all my heart. Because he loves me. I pray, he answers; if I do wrong, I confess to him and he forgives me and makes me pure as he is pure.

A UNIVERSITY STUDENT:
Thank you for coming to Cambodia to teach Khmer people. I must tell you about my old life

6

The Great One Has Come

God has more than one means of waking people who have been sleeping long enough and who need to heed his alarm.

Christmas 1971. The Khmer church was still more or less a nonentity. But the leaders decided they wanted to explain and to share with their countrymen the true meaning of Christmas. Their plan? Try to rent the big new auditorium on the waterfront in Phnom Penh. But would the government consent, would they give permission for such a meeting to be held? They did. Praise God.

A huge sign in front of the auditorium announced:

THE GREAT ONE HAS BEEN BORN—
THE GREAT ONE HAS COME.

The building was crammed full for the meeting, with three times as many turned away. What drew the huge crowd? Whether the Khmer Christian leaders had this in mind or not, who knows, but there is in their heritage a prophecy that says, "During a time of war, a 'great one, a god' would come to the place where four rivers meet, with scars in his hands, his feet, and side."

It was a time of war. The place was literally "where four rivers meet." The people had lost their king who was, to them, more than part deity. They were subjects without a king, sheep without a shepherd. And heartbreak was their daily companion.

"The prophet will be Cambodia's deliverer," the prophecy declared. What better time to share the Good News of Christmas? Especially when we combine with the circumstances the ancient Cambodian proverb, "When blood flows, the heart grows softer."

Gene Hall reported that even high officials were inquiring, "Who is this God?"

That was the first attempt by the national Christians themselves to come out of their corner. The missionaries had been permitted to return and had done so at the invitation of the Khmers themselves. When government restrictions against American missionaries were lifted, Dr. L. L. King, after consulting in Hong Kong with the missionaries concerned, sat down with the church leaders in Phnom Penh and listened as they discussed whether or not they wanted the foreign missionary and if so, which ones and for what specific purposes. He gave them twenty-four hours to come to a decision. Five years of enforced missionary absence had demonstrated to the nationals the areas in which they still needed assistance. Nevertheless, the Cambodian church had started to grow up. The Christmas undertaking was this church beginning to emerge from the shadows.

FOURTH-YEAR ENGINEERING STUDENT:
Since I have studied this Bible course I have a
great love for God in my heart. In the past I was
jealous and proud. Today God has corrected me.
I think of Romans 5:1, "So now, since we have
been made right in God's sight by faith in his
promises, we can have real peace with him
because of what Jesus Christ our Lord has done
for us." Man dies. I am a man, so I die. My
body is composed of organic matter—so my life
is temporary. I do not inherit eternal life, but
God intervened and sent his Son in order that
we might receive the gift of the immortal and
eternal life.

A high school senior who studied once a week in
the English Bible classes wrote, after a couple of
months, expressing his personal search for peace.

I'm Just Loving
Sometimes, before I study the Bible, I used to
ask myself and other people, Must I believe in
God? But now I am just finding the answer.
People for a long time used to ask me, Who is
our ancestor? At first I did not know. I tried to
research its answer in all the books that I know.
One science book tells me that men come from
monkeys. It is one idea. But I doubt it, for if we
know we come from a monkey, who is the
monkey's ancestor? So it is all in vain. We don't
know again!
    One day it was very wonderful when I started
to learn the Gospel of John. After that, I know
that all things in the world—*and the world
itself*—are created by God.
        So we know that our first Ancestor is God!
Who is God?

God is not a man, for he lived before the world or heaven were created. By John I know that God is Spirit. So God can be everywhere. But that is not all. We want to know God's heart. How can we know God's heart? We must know one man, God's Son, Jesus Christ. No one can approach to his goodness, for we are sinners. We do not have a clean heart. But does not Jesus perform miracles? His first miracle was changing water into wine. So we know he can change sinners into great men. That is not all. He died on the cross of wood to save people from the darkness of sin and death; from illness, hunger and bad belief.

The greatest work of Jesus, I think, is dying for us. Because our biggest flaw is sin. It is terrible for us. No one can save us from our sin but Jesus. Oh, Lord, now I'm just loving you—now I'm just loving.

Having crawled into the hearts and minds of these Christian brothers and sisters, having listened to their expressions of what Jesus and the Word of God mean in their lives, surely we can trust these Khmer Christians to be God's people, come what may.

Because it was evident that the Khmer Christians themselves were at the forefront of this venture, they were refuting the accusations that they were, as Prince Sihanouk had scathingly called some, "candy Christians"; they were demonstrating that they were not just servants of the Americans, embracing a foreigner's religion, but that they were themselves truly following the God in whom they had come to believe, and that they were still true Cambodians.

Who can question that it was the Spirit of God who led these men to choose this daring new approach, this timely announcement, at this particular place! God encouraged the church to "go public."

Some have asked, How much did the later mass crusades, the "American-type evangelism," influence the spiritual upsurge in Cambodia? I would not presume to have the answer, though, like everyone else, I have given this much thought. Common sense would indicate that these crusades were a determining factor, that they did indeed play their role in the phenomenon. For an understanding of how important they were, one would in my opinion need to know a great deal about the Buddhist mentality.

For balance, it's good to remember that the national church was beginning to move in this direction and make Christianity less obscure than it had been for fifty years. In the vanguard was Major Chhirc and Minh Thien Voan; with them on the planning committee for the Christmas impact was Merle Graven.

That same Christmas, in another part of the city, the Monivang church had gone all out with a program which government officials attended. Here too, many more people came than there was room to accommodate. Louisa Graven had, at the church's request, worked long and hard with the children's choir, the youth choir, and "specials" that honored Christ and touched hearts.

With this emergence of Christianity, it was all the more significant when in April 1970 Dr. Stan Mooneyham rode at the front of a convoy of relief goods along the dangerous Da Nang trail from Saigon into Phnom Penh. He preceded any returning American missionaries. In Phnom Penh when Dr. Mooneyham arrived were the Rev. and Mrs. Jean Fune and Mr. and Mrs. Jacques Piaget of the Alliance Chretianne Mission. With Mooneyham's coming, spiritual teaching was teaming up with practical help (not that the missionaries had not been wholly compassionate and helped in many ways; but the World Vision project was a big, visible, clear-cut "We're bringing food and clothing and medicine to help you" in the name of Christ).

Much publicity was given by the media; the name and the face of Dr. Stan Mooneyham began to be equated with the foreigners' religion which until then had not been too visible. What Mooneyham did caused people to take a second look at the Christians—*was what this one American was doing, part of what these others had been saying for fifty years?* It's understandable, then, that when World Vision came in with a gospel team in addition to their help for the myriad human problems, they had a ready-made audience. It must not be overlooked (as we've mentioned elsewhere) that it was the *national* Christians whom the crowds heard. It was a national, Son Sonne, a fellow Cambodian, who as interpreter gave them the message of Jesus Christ. They could never have understood it in English (some individuals would have, but not the masses).

What was it like, this three-day "American-type" evangelistic crusade?

Phnom Penh's largest auditorium was rented. The
C & MA Field Chairman describes the event:

"Can you imagine such a thing happening a few
years ago? 'Every high-ranking official received a
personal invitation!'

"Then came Friday, April 14, the day toward which
we had worked and prayed. The Danniebelle Singers
had appeared on television; 2,000 posters had been
placed throughout the city; 30,000 handbills had been
distributed; and ads had appeared in newspapers for
five days. But what would be the response to this first
evangelistic effort of three days? The service was to
begin at 4:00 P.M. The military police should have
been present by 2:00 P.M., but they were late in
arriving. By 2:30, the crowds began to gather. The
MP's arrived. A quick search was made of the
building, and at 3:05, the gate to the fence
surrounding the auditorium was opened. By then so
many had gathered that they nearly stampeded the
MPs in endeavoring to get to the auditorium,
prohibiting a thorough "frisking" as required by law.
[Why the frisking? Some time earlier a number of
Communists created a disturbance at a crowded public
event; this diversion made it possible for frogmen to
sabotage a major bridge and three ships—Author]. By
3:20, the auditorium was packed and more than 100
were still en route between the gate of the fence and
the auditorium door. The door was locked and the
people outside refused to depart but demanded
entrance. We were frightened by the threat of a riot.
Finally, it was agreed that those already on the
compound could enter the auditorium but must stand
around the sides. An estimated 4,000 to 6,000 were
turned away on the first day.

"The seventy-voice choir opened the service at

exactly 4:00. Dr. Mooneyham was then introduced, receiving a warm applause. He, in turn, introduced the Danniebelles. Unlike most stateside services, everything was applauded, even the reading of the Scripture and prayer! Stan gave a simple but pointed message stressing the new life in Christ.

"As World Vision reporter, Billy Bray, wrote (May 1972):

> In his messages Mooneyham shucked the highly embroidered style of much American evangelism for a simple teaching approach. He carefully told the story of Jesus Christ; for most of the audience it was the first time they had ever heard about him.
>
> Mooneyham said afterwards that he had never preached like he did during the crusade. "There was no embellishment and few illustrations. It was just a simple, unvarnished presentation of the Good News about Jesus Christ. I felt like an announcer rather than a preacher."

"As he came to the climax, he asked, 'Do you want this new life?' Unexpectedly a roar sounded throughout the building—YES! Stan asked that those stand who desired to receive this new life in Christ. Four to five hundred stood. Unbelievable. They must have misunderstood. The terms were then made difficult. You may be mocked, ridiculed, expelled from your home. Think it over. Then if you still mean it, please come forward. Without hesitation, this great body of people moved to the front with an undertone of voices as they came. We wondered, Could they be serious? Or might they be planning a riot? They were admonished by Mooneyham, then prayed for. The service was dismissed with instructions for those who had come to the front of but a handful of converts we were still considered less than nobodies; at the best, perhaps, exponents of a foreign religion that was making no inroads on the Khmer people; at the worst, the somewhat inept enemies of Buddhism. And the crusades did much to change all that, to give Christianity a clearly focused, positive image." For the missionaries and the national believers it was like living in the eye of a miracle! After fifty long years.

One of the greatest and most long-range effects came from the distribution of literature to interested individuals. Said Norman Ens: "During the second crusade, we gave to each of the 2,600 who came forward to accept Christ, Lesson 1 of the Gospel of John, along with other booklets. About 100 returned the completed lesson, indicating that the others may not have been serious seekers at that time—but it did get the literature into their hands."

Dr. Mooneyham underscored this literature impact:

> Not a few Buddhist monks have expressed an interest in the gospel, and at least one I know about has put off his robes and embraced Christ. Every Buddhist priest studying at the university has received a Bible. Bible distribution by the Bible Society and the Gideons has outstripped the financial ability of the local Christians to supply them. We have just given $10,000, which will be matched by the Bible societies, to replenish the stock.
>
> I see no signs of a let-up in the spiritual interest, and I believe we are going to see an unprecedented response when the war is over. You see, many of the new converts are refugees who will return to their homes when the rural areas are secure. They will be like sparks

scattered abroad. This prospect causes me to
tingle.[1]

In this connection I'm reminded of a conversation I
had with a thoughtful young Britisher, Tony Harrob.
Interested in training nationals, he had worked for
some time with Operation Mobilization and was then
teaching in Dacca University in Bangladesh. With a
few days off school, he came to my writing seminar in
Chandpur, and as we were discussing the situation in
Cambodia (between sessions) he shared this thinking.
He saw a parallel between the new Christians "in the
first flush of fervor" and the endangered Christians in
Jerusalem in apostolic times. "They're so many, and
it's been so impossible to get them all organized into
churches as fast as they believed, that as a group they
will be difficult to identify and therefore may not be
singled out for persecution. The crisis situation just
could be God's way of scattering them all over, taking
the gospel with them."

I found myself agreeing and praying all the more.

The crusades may have served in a figurative sense
as a "day of Pentecost." Unquestionably, of the
3,000 who believed in Jesus on that historic day,
some had, earlier, some exposure to who Jesus was
and what he had done. They may have been among
the crowds to whom John the Baptist preached;
perhaps they were on the fringes when Jesus
performed a miracle; some might even have lunched
on the miracle bread and fish on the mountainside.
Peter's fervent preaching in the power of the Holy
Spirit must have awakened memories, aroused and
then dispelled long-lingering doubts. Likewise, in
Cambodia's capital, among those who thronged to the

[1] Stan Mooneyham, from *World Vision.* Used by permission of World
Vision.

the auditorium to advance to the platform for further counseling, literature, and more prayer. They still responded, and it was then that the counselors divided them into groups of five and eight, so each one's name, address, age, profession, etc., could be recorded on a card and then dealt with as thoroughly as possible. It was nearly 7:00 P.M. when all was finished. We were numb with excitement and astonishment. And physically exhausted.

"To avoid complete disappointment and not turn the crowds away on the remaining two days, we requested permission to erect a platform and install mikes outside the auditorium, but within the fenced area, and also requested that the overflow crowd be permitted to enter this section but remain outside the auditorium. It was a calculated risk. Would they depart or demand entrance and cause a riot, for they had nearly broken windows in the auditorium the day before and one door was torn from its hinges by the over 100 people previously mentioned. Before 3:30, the auditorium was again filled to capacity. The doors were locked. The people continued to come. A few minutes before 4:00 the Danniebelles began to sing to the crowd outside while the choir opened the service at 4:00 on the inside. After two or three numbers, the Danniebelles went inside to continue the service there while Stan spoke to 4,000 on the outside. A wonderful response followed a brief message by Stan, and the counselors went to work. Apart from those who remained to receive the Savior, the crowd dispersed orderly and peacefully. The service in the auditorium closed with another tremendous response to the short and simple appeal to put their trust in the only God who could save them.

"The closing day found some 2,000 outside while the auditorium was again filled to capacity. In both places, the response to the message, 'The End of the World' was terrific. Here is the breakdown of those responding:

	University Students	High School Students	Military	Others	Total
Received Christ	46	424	70	94	634
Inquirers	53	197	46	73	369

"Subsequent to the above figures, twenty more cards were turned in by counselors indicating an additional twenty who prayed for salvation. Four of the Cambodian churches in the Phnom Penh area benefited in attendance due to the Mooneyham Crusade."

As part of the follow-up, Lim Chheong ("the idol-maker's son"), director of the Bible school, invited those who had filled out decision cards to attend a special service at the Bible school from 2:30 to 3:30 the next day. As he gave out the invitations, some asked, "May we bring our friends?" To everyone's amazement around 300 responded, and from among the "friends" sixty accepted Christ.

No one, missionary or national Christian, would ever dispute the value of these crusades. To the day that the last missionary had to leave Phnom Penh, people were still coming to receive the Lord and some were saying, "I first heard at the crusade."

While the church did not "triple" as has been suggested by some spectators, the crusades did have the effect of "putting Christianity on the map," as Gene Hall stated and other missionaries on the scene concurred. What these missionaries were saying is this: "We've been plugging along for years, and by all

"Yes, if I can use the Bible to teach. If you want me on that basis, I'll come." A day later they replied, "We definitely want you to come." One week the lesson was in Matthew 4, dealing with repentance. Merle asked the men what that meant and among the many answers one was, "Sin is disobedience to God!" Merle went on, "Is there anyone here who feels he has never sinned?" In one great chorus they shouted him down, "No!"

It was hard for the missionary to believe such directness was now a reality.

Speaking of a trip he made back to Cambodia where he had served for nine years, Clifford Westergren said, "Everywhere I looked, everything I heard was throbbing with spiritual expectancy. It seemed that even God was excited about Cambodia. Certain spiritual realities stood out . . . I went to Cambodia tired, but I returned home refreshed."

Cliff spoke also of the Chinese church in Phnom Penh (a special interest since he is a missionary now in Hong Kong). At the Chinese church, though they had lost 120 members to Hong Kong and Singapore, there was no sense of discouragement or resignation. The picture Cliff saw was: Two Sunday schools, one in Chinese, one in English—seven young people committed to the Lord's service—four choirs—the purchase of a Volkswagen bus when personal incomes were at an all-time low—the steady leadership of Miriam Ho and Daniel Lam. A work not without problems, but these are hidden beneath an abiding presence of hope and expectancy.

In summing up this ten-day trip to Cambodia, Mr. Westergren said, "During my short visit I learned directly of five who had just received Jesus as their Savior. Only too well can I remember how we would have rejoiced *if that number represented a yearly report!*"

The seed had been planted in those earlier days. And because seed has life in it, it had not died. For long years it had just appeared to be lifeless.

Among the factors God used in the upsurge of new life were the crusades sponsored by World Vision. They unquestionably brought the focus of public attention to the Christian faith. They thereby helped to make it possible for both national believers and missionaries to do a more effective work than was possible when the church was for one reason or another "hiding its light under a bushel."

We will not quote more statistics. Statistics are necessary in their place, but they're not very inspiring. What does inspire and encourage us is not the numbers of persons who made decisions for Christ, but what happened in their lives and in the lives of others because of their decision.

The missionaries who had plugged on in the face of every kind of opposition must have often rubbed their eyes to make sure they were quite awake and not just dreaming what was happening.

It became obvious that the method didn't really matter. Whether it was one-to-one evangelism, mass crusades, radio broadcasts, Bible classes, English classes, or correspondence courses, the fruit was ripe for the picking. As one missionary insisted, "It was God giving the people a heart to believe." God's clock was striking Cambodia's hour, and no force could stop it!

Said Malcolm Bradshaw, who was studying church growth in Asia, "We are seeing a place where Christianity is fresh and new. It is not often that you're able to see Christianity begin. We are on the threshhold of the whole thing."[2]

[2]*World Vision*, May 1972.

crusades we can believe that some, perhaps many, did
have a background for listening. They had been
exposed to some Christian literature; they had known
someone who had turned from Buddhism to serve the
living Christ. And—who can say—since syncretism
had watered down and defiled the pure Buddhist
doctrines, bringing in animal sacrifices, were some
suffering from a violated conscience? Were they
searching for the One who can forgive sins?

Or was it that when trouble came and they couldn't
handle it they became humble, thus putting
themselves in line for God's mercies, and the large
public meeting offered an opportunity?

The second crusade, November 1972, featured the
inimitable Palermo Brothers and Dr. Mooneyham.

"These singers received more invitations to appear
in schools than we could fill," read a report to
C & MA headquarters. "This in itself is a new turn
for the Khmer Republic. Likewise, the Palermos
were given forty minutes on TV the night before the
crusade began. About five minutes before the end of
the program, President Lon Nol phoned the station
requesting them to continue. With their customary
enthusiasm the brothers Phil and Louie played and
dedicated to the President of Cambodia, "If God Be
for Us, Who Can Be against Us?"

One of the surprising things to the national
Christians was that so many of their own people were
so willing to accept Jesus as their Savior. The small
pockets of believers, as they became participants in
this wide-open evangelistic effort and saw its effect on
their own countrymen, expanded their spiritual
horizons. They began to believe for all of Cambodia!

"We began to find out," Marie Ens told me, "that
no matter what the new Christian's background or
profession, we could introduce him to someone,

another Christian, who 'matched.' This is extremely important in a culture where religion determines almost every other area of life.

This acceptance of Christianity on many levels of society added a whole new dimension to the stature of the Khmer church. They began to have acceptance as a viable piece of Cambodian society—something the early missionaries, while they had this dream, probably never envisioned in their wildest imaginings (or possibly even in their earnest praying). Khmer Christians having standing in the community, in hyper Buddhist Cambodia!

An example of the recognition of Christians was when on one occasion the Protestant church was invited to a large conference supporting the U.N. resolution seeking for peace. All religious bodies were to present papers, so the conference gave the evangelical church opportunity to share its concern for peace and to inform the conference that they were praying to God towards this end.

In 1974, the church was very public. Gene Hall wrote his Mission Board, ''CHRISTMAS PROGRAM AT THE STADIUM: The Khmer Evangelical Church has special programs on December 24 and 25 at the Olympic Stadium. Sixteen churches had booths depicting stories in the Bible in sequence from Genesis to Revelation. It proved most effective. Around 6,000 to 8,000 people attended both days, among them the mayor of Phnom Penh and other VIPs. The results are difficult to measure, but we believe all things have their place.''

The effect of the recognition of Christianity to a degree was that the missionary felt more personal freedom. For instance, according to a report by Cliff Westergren, Merle Graven was requested to teach English to the heads of the National Bank. His reply:

The Lord's Work Walks On

A question that engaged many participants at the International Congress on World Evangelization (Lausanne, 1974), was, "Where does the Church find sufficient leadership for new congregations?"

Sitting in that auditorium with the rest of us was a man who is himself an answer to this question: Mr. Son Sonne of the Khmer Republic. We will hear more of him.

In his plenary paper, *"The Church as God's Agent of Evangelism,"* Mr. Howard A. Snyder of Sao Paulo, Brazil, addressed himself to this matter of finding leadership:

> The answer to this question [leadership for new congregations] is found in the fact of spiritual gifts and in the community life of the church. If we live with our brethren in true Christian

community and if we expect the Spirit to provide the necessary spiritual gifts, the right gifts of leadership will appear at the right time to take care of the demands of growth . . . when the Church is truly the community of God's people, it is *God the Spirit* who provides the necessary leadership. This is his promise to us (Romans 16:1).

Almost as though he were describing the situation in Cambodia, Snyder expanded his statement:

The way to biblical evangelism today is to bring each believer to discover and use his spiritual gifts. When this happens, not only does evangelism occur, but there is also *a valid Christian community* to welcome new converts and *a valid Christian life-style* of faith and good works that creates no credibility gap with the world.

Speaking of comparatively new Christians who launched out for God, practically every missionary remarked on the converts' amazing perception and comprehension of spiritual truth. Nurse Barbara Neath, with her warm Yorkshire accent, said, "I have never known anything like it before and I think I shall never see it again; they seemed to have insight beyond what some of us older Christians ever have. This is the most outstanding impression I gained in Cambodia."

"It's more than knowledge," another remarked, "it's a gift from the Lord."

"It's the Spirit of the Lord moving through the land, a fresh breeze," suggests Dr. Dean Kroh, "and we're seeing young Christians assuming positions of leadership; it's amazing; one who has been saved just two or three months is out winning souls!"

"We were the hidden people," said Mr. Chau, president of the Cambodian Evangelical Church, "but now we are visible."

The Great One had come—and Phnom Penh was sitting up and taking notice.

itself must have been enough to attract some people,
make them hunger for the source of such gladness.
And they were *single-hearted.* Think what this must
have done for them! For when we are totally
engrossed with someone (some*thing,* at times) nothing
else and nothing less can really affect us; we can ride
the waves and roll with the punches.

History has always borne this out. The dedicated,
single-hearted soldier, scientist, athlete, missionary,
and individual Christian can withstand almost
anything, so totally absorbed are they with what has
captured their vision and their allegiance. I see this as
explaining these Cambodian Christians, almost
impatient with anything else—war, hunger, an
uncertain future for their country. They were totally
caught up in God's program, absorbed with their
newfound faith.

Personally I have never known any of the trauma
that surrounds such situations as the Cambodians and
the Vietnamese and others have had to face (though
as the mother of a missionary in Bangladesh, I
agonized over their special horrors).

I do know from personal experience the joy that
floods our lives when we're single-hearted toward
Jesus Christ. Saved out of a less than nominally
religious background, I was fortunate to get in with a
small group of fervent believers, most of them, like
myself, untaught in the Scriptures. But we had good
times learning together. An instance that comes to
mind is when one of us wanted to find a certain verse
in the New Testament. We hadn't a clue where to
find it. Using the brains the Lord had given us (even
though we didn't know the Bible), we divided the
New Testament among us and each went on a verse
hunt. We eventually discovered that the verse we
were searching for isn't in the Bible—not in the form

we had in mind—but we read a lot and we had such treasures to share with each other as we too went from house to house.

It's no mystery to me, then, that God can take new, young Christians, real "babes" and use them. It's the Holy Spirit who teaches and guides us into all truth. Now, lest I leave anyone with the false impression that I am not for Christian training and education, let me say that I most definitely am. Jesus thoroughly trained his corps of witnesses for three years. And every reputable missionary and missionary organization has as a major thrust the training of nationals after winning them to Christ. Even so, God is not locked into gear so that he cannot be omnipotent in every situation. Cambodia in these past few years and especially in the final months of missionary endeavor there, is one of God's Exhibit A's of what he can do in the lives of people who are wholeheartedly his, and who are single-hearted toward him. He can make sure that his work walks on.

Nevertheless, God uses people.

To quote Cliff Westergren, who with his wife and family served for nine years in Cambodia, and while he has the supervision of the Alliance Press in Hong Kong is an ardent Cambodia watcher: "In looking for keys to the spiritual upsurge in Cambodia, we must never overlook the leadership of the older pastors. For example, new Christians were sent to these seven pastors who sat down with them and counseled with them. This afforded the converts excellent opportunity to clarify what conversion to Christ is and what their decision to follow him entails. The pastor would then give the new convert a copy of one of the Gospels, tell him to read it, and then come back with his questions. This was a Cambodian being nurtured

"I've been a Christian for a long, long time," a young Cambodian said. The long time? *Six months*—and he felt a strong sense of responsibility to share his faith, and he was doing it.

Why should we be amazed at this?

On my recent mission to a number of countries, I admit to having had to mentally hurdle something of the same observed spiritual depth on the part of the national Christians. Working with Lao, Thai, and Bengali believers, I was in a new way impressed with their relationship to Christ, their knowledge of the Word of God, and their ability to apply the Scriptures to their lives. In workshop sessions they wrote in their own language, and it was as their writings were translated for me that I learned just how very much understanding they had, and how deep is their commitment to Jesus Christ. I was blessed and inspired in my soul. The result was that I found myself analyzing a certain arrogance, a Western smugness, that had (albeit subconsciously) made me feel surprised that the Holy Spirit could be in such measure in non-English speaking Christians. I asked the Lord to forgive me.

This soul-searching made me rethink something missionary Tom Wisley had remarked in an interview we had following his evacuation from Phnom Penh. Speaking of the earlier occasion when American missionaries had to pull out of Cambodia (when Prince Sihanouk had ousted them all in 1965), Tom shared his thinking:

"The church was left on its own, had to find its own way, had to decide whether they would throw the whole Christian thing over. Some did, but some did not; and these became strong in faith and in character, became better persons because of it. They now had to make their own decisions instead of having the missionaries decide things for them. My personal opinion is that the best thing that could have happened to the church in Cambodia at that time was this removal of the foreign missionaries. If this could happen in all mission countries—say, evacuation for a time," Tom postulated, "the church caused to stand on its own feet, I think we would see some things that might surprise us; it might not be as bad as we tend to fear it would be. It comes back to the truth of Ephesians: it's Christ's church. He is the Head" (and I found myself adding "and the gates of hell shall not prevail against it").

The Lord's work *will* walk on.

Why should we feel any wonder, why do some of us view such leadership with a cautious "wait and see" attitude? Maybe we're even a little doubtful that God really knows what he's doing. Maybe we would like to take the Holy Spirit aside and offer a little twentieth-century counsel on the basis of our findings.

It occurs to me that the Book of Acts does not record anything about a follow-up committee, a corps of trained counselors, on the Day of Pentecost with its harvest of 3,000 new believers to be cared for. Who took down their names, addresses, religious affiliation, etc? Oh, there was follow-up! And there were prayer meetings (attended by Peter and the other disciples when they weren't in jail or otherwise occupied in the precarious business of defending the gospel in those days).

One thing we are told is that there was *lots of fellowship.* Two other things characterized that early group of Christians, two beautiful things: *gladness*—they were happy, joyous people; that in

Typical Cambodian frame house. The thatched building at the right houses a refugee family.

Inset: Refugee child.

The throne building at the royal palace in Phnom Pehn.
Inset: Cambodian lumber mill. Most lumber is still hand sawn and planed.

Central railroad station in Phnom Pehn.

Inset: Christian girl's face reflects hope even in dark days of war.

Ta Khman Bible School, which provided theological training for national pastors. Dormitory at right, with open-air chapel at left.

Inset: Youth choir in a Christian church.

The home of the Cambodian director of the Ta Khman Bible School.

Left inset: Dr. Dean Kroh ministers to a patient in one of the C and M. A. refugee camps.

Center inset: Tirah, a Bible school graduate, witnesses to a leprosy patient in her home.

Right inset: C. and M. A. missionary Ruth Patterson distributes tracts in a refugee settlement.

Christian hospital built in Phnom Pehn by World Vision. It was to have been administered by C. and M. A. staff, but before it could be opened or dedicated, the country fell to insurgent forces.

Inset: In rural areas, water must be carried from the village well.

War leaves its cruel mark upon undernourished children in Cambodia.

Below: Refugee child receiving daily portion of rice for his family.

in his faith by a fellow Cambodian, a mature
Christian.

"Also, God supplied just the right auxiliary
personnel, e.g. World Vision with its ministry of
compassion, in practical demonstration. World Vision
played a major role."

"The city-wide crusades put Christianity on the
map in Cambodia," states Norman Ens. "That's
when the church got really widespread publicity, on
TV, and posters—real exposure. This is without
question where scores and scores of people had their
first introduction to Christianity—the Mooneyham
Crusades. Take Sin Som, for example. He was one of
those who raised their hands in the meeting. There
was a real moving of the Spirit in the church one
evening, and we used the same format as the
Canadian revival with the chairs around and one chair
in the middle. I remember very, very definitely Sin
Som kneeling at that chair and weeping and pouring
out his heart to the Lord, begging forgiveness. 'That's
the time I really repented,' he's told me often. 'At
the crusade I went along with everyone else because I
did want new life in Christ, but I didn't know what
repentance was.'

"I think," says Norman thoughtfully, "this was the
case with a lot of folk who went up to the front. Even
so, the meetings had great value and I wouldn't say
there were not genuine conversions; there were."

Visiting evangelists and pastors and Bible teachers
can likewise be credited with doing much to foster
the spiritual explosion. The cultural tie between
Cambodia and India made particularly effective the
ministry of Indian brethren. Rev. Chavin, Augustine
Salins, and Ben Wati are remembered for their
contribution, as is Ravi Zacharias. Missionaries told
C & MA headquarters in New York:

Ravi's youth, nationality, and obvious anointing of the Spirit gained immediate entrance into the hearts of the people . . . Often we tend to perpetuate the old, but there was something fresh in this dynamic, eloquent, and Spirit-filled Indian. They received him as one of them. It has been thrilling to see people from all walks of life seek Christ; last week, a major in charge of the military radio station; yesterday a professor in the university, along with two Buddhist monks. The major who wrote the National Anthem, himself a new Christian, brought his wife and nine students to the meetings, and all of them responded to the invitation to receive Christ. There were 660 decisions for Christ. Not only were souls saved but individual churches were electrified, for this was the very first evangelistic meeting for some of the new churches . . .

The harvest is so ripe that no longer is there the need for plucking, but rather for gathering the fruit that has fallen of its own accord.

Another report of the spontaneous response phrased it this way:

It reminds us of the Day of Pentecost—3,000 responded under the ministry of Peter, but the account does not stop there; the Lord added daily to the church such as should be saved.

Among others God has used was a three-man team from the *Logos,* the Operation Mobilization ship. Their gung ho attitude toward literature distribution and witnessing matched that of the zealous young Khmer Christians themselves.

Campus Crusade for Christ likewise made its

impact in training the new Christians in methods of
outreach to their own people.

During the fifth Khmer Rouge offensive in
February [1975], a young staff couple of Khmer
Campus Crusade for Christ were able, together with
their new converts, to expose 531 people to the
message of Christ; 345 (or 65 percent) of these
responded and invited Christ into their hearts.

Virtually untouched with the gospel (97.5 percent
Buddhist until three years earlier) the Khmer
Republic has seen such widespread turning to Christ
in recent months that the local newspapers began to
call for government containment of Christianity. This
staff couple are also heavily involved in translating
Campus Crusade's basic materials for evangelism and
discipleship into the Khmer language.[1]

A group greatly appreciated was the five OMF
missionaries who entered the Khmer Republic in 1974
and made an impact for the Lord. They assisted in the
Bible school, directed the Christian Youth Center and
also taught many Bible classes. They were dearly
loved and led many people to Christ. Some of this
group have continued to carry on a ministry to the
Khmer people in refugee camps in the United States
and other areas.

Then there were the Gideons and the Bible
Society, truly God's servants to the churches.

Thus in many ways the Lord worked by his Holy
Spirit and through the lives of Christians who were
listening to his voice, whose hearts God turned to
Cambodia. This is one answer to Howard Snyder's
question at Lausanne: "Where does the Church find
sufficient leadership for new congregations?"

It's a good question. But had a layman such as Mr.

[1]Adapted from *Asian Campus Crusade* magazine, April 1975.

Son Sonne of Cambodia allowed himself to be caught up in the question rather than himself becoming part of the answer, we would not be able to report the Book of Acts happenings of which he was a major part.

Meanwhile, the missionaries on the scene had learned the lesson of history and they were concentrating on training and teaching the nationals.

Said C & MA's Norman Ens: "We realized the situation was getting worse and worse all the time. We weren't packing any suitcases—never did any packing at all, as a matter of fact. One thing we did do, however, we did try to actively train someone who could take our responsibility. For instance, I'm in literature work, and last April the church selected a young Bible school student, an extremely trustworthy young man, to be their representative in the literature field. From the time I got him in May, I just did everything to train him so that he would know my field.

"My wife is in Sunday school work and she had been training Sunday school teachers. She had a counterpart, a Cambodian who had learned so much that the whole Sunday school ministry was turned over to her. It's really great to see people who have taken the reins and are going ahead; the work is not slowing down at all.

"The missionaries' ministry in the past four and a half years since we were permitted to come back has been a teaching ministry: Bible School and TEE (Theological Education by Extension); Bible studies in churches and in the Youth Center, in Cambodian and in English. When you look at it, it's been teaching, teaching, teaching all the time."

Mrs. Ens added, "There's been a real hunger on the part of the new Christians to learn. We had forty

in the TEE program, coming three days a week from
3:00 to 6:00 P.M. These were mostly grown men, not
young people, and they were giving nine hours a
week to the study of the Bible, which shows how
hungry they were to go on with the Lord and really
know what their Christianity is supposed to mean to
them.

"TEE took on a new look one night. One of the
students brought some unsaved friends to monitor the
class. One gave his heart to the Savior at the
conclusion of the study. Forty-one were present,
although not all are enrolled.

"Not so much was happening with the women,"
Marie Ens explained. "In the evangelistic meetings
some would respond, but there isn't much work by
women for women. The women are definitely far
below men in their position and their value in
Cambodian society. For instance, it's their highest
hope that in the next reincarnation, they would
possibly be men. So the women are not considered
important and their ideas are not important. When a
man becomes a Christian, he feels a responsibility to
see that his wife goes along, and I think that this has
often been the case—the man believing and his wife
just following along rather than believing
independently for herself. One thing I tried with the
Bible school students was a class for young women
and I tried to help them understand *their own worth*
before the Lord; that this is something Christianity
offers; that the Lord loves his daughters as much as he
loves his sons.

"As far as taking leadership in the home," Marie
was quick to add, "that is the man's place, but it's
not that God loves the fellows more than he loves the
girls. I enjoyed it very much that I could share with

them that Christianity has this to tell the women. Buddhism doesn't have it for them."

The training paid off, for in letters reaching them after their evacuation, Norman and Marie had the joy of reading, "The Lord's work walks on like it always did."

What is it costing some of the Khmer believers to stand for God? Are they exhibiting what *Time* correspondent David Aikman commented on while we drank coffee in Hong Kong: "I saw in Cambodia a spiritual depth, a maturity, a stability and expectation of persecution—and a willingness to face it."

Later, Mr. Aikman amplified this for me. "There's a belief that in spite of what is going on, *God is in control*. This is the affirmative conclusion of the Cambodian pastors whose evangelistic work is most likely to be directly curtailed by a Khmer Rouge victory in Cambodia. So far nothing has been heard of the Christian communities which have fallen under Communist control. No one is optimistic about committed Christians who fall into the hands of the Khmer Rouge, for Cambodia's Communists by most accounts seem to be more brutal and less disciplined than the Vietcong and the North Vietnamese. But the handwriting is on the wall. One prominent pastor received an anonymous note last week threatening his life if and when the Khmer Rouge enter Phnom Penh. Another, Pastor Son Sonne, 36, regarded as the leader of the Khmer Evangelical Church, has no illusions about the fate likely to await him after a Communist victory: 'I know for sure that if they come they will stop and arrest me.' Concurs Pastor Nou-Thay, 'My motive is to serve the Lord or die.' "

The following letter speaks for itself as to another Christian leader's determination.

Phnom Penh
April 7, 1975

Dear Mr. Hall,

Jesus is alive, isn't he? And so are we over here
in Phnom Penh amid rockets, electricity, and
food shortage.

Please remember to pray for our International
Church every Sunday at 5 P.M. at Bethany
Church. The service is going on as the Lord is
willing.

Today we failed to have our hospital
dedication service. The Lord willing, the work
there is carried on. Please continue to ask God
to bless us and his work among the Khmer
people as a whole. Much work as you know has
to be done. The Lord is with us, isn't he? This is
according to John 14:18. And we praise him
because we are *not on the losing side*!

Many souls are so hungry for God's Word.
Please pray for us as we keep on serving him in
all circumstances. May hundreds of thousands of
souls be saved by the grace of our Lord Jesus
Christ.

From the talk I last had with you on Thursday
night in Phnom Penh, would you please pray for
me that I may not forget Philippians 1:21. "For
me to live is Christ, and to die is gain" (RSV).

The Lord bless you all.

Your servant in the Lord,

God is using this caliber of Christian in his church
in Cambodia to walk on as usual. Major Chhirc knew
he might be called to die for Christ. "I have studied
communism," he told Gene Hall. "Communists are

willing to die for what they believe. Is not Jesus worth more than they!''

"In many respects," adds David Aikman, "the Cambodian church is well prepared. The rapid growth has led most Christians to become accustomed to leadership from lay people, a situation that is bound to develop in Cambodia if most of the leaders of the church are indeed arrested as seems likely. Second, a consignment of Khmer-language Bibles was recently imported, more than enough for all the believers presently in the country. Last, those who have radios will be able to hear Khmer-language Christian broadcasting from the Manila-based Far East Broadcasting Company.

"Intriguingly, there is a strong belief among many Cambodian pastors and laymen that communism will, ultimately, serve the Christian message in Cambodia, as many Christians believe it has already done in China. Those who hold this view point out that communism usually creates good internal communications and stamps out superstitious beliefs faster than any other political system, a step forward in Christian eyes. Son Sonne puts it this way: 'Communism is sweeping away idolatry.'

"Since Cambodia is a highly devout Buddhist nation with a strong admixture of spiritism, Son Sonne's argument, from his own standpoint, is valid. Moreover, pastor Todd Burke, whose phenomenal success in two years might have rendered him reluctant to see all the fruits of his labors submerged by the rolling tide of a new ideology, waxes almost enthusiastic about the probable Khmer Rouge triumph in Cambodia. 'We are ready,' he says. 'I believe that once we leave and the Communists take over, evangelization is just going to expand explosively in Cambodia.' ''

Persecution. Fiery trials. Imprisonment. Death. Historically, suffering and repression such as this has been the seed from which has sprung a strong church. It's not enough, however, for us to glory in the courage of Christian martyrs half a world away. These are our *brethren*. It should take the sleep from our eyes and drive us to our knees even though we can only speculate as to what is happening to them.

By compassion and practical aid toward the refugees—Christian and not-yet-Christian refugees—and by unceasing prayer, we can each have a part as the Lord's church walks on in Cambodia.

8

Heartbreak and Triumph

Nurse Mary Lou Rorabaugh's voice was tense with emotion. "I had to drive away from camp at sundown, knowing that my very favorite little boy in that camp was going to be dead by morning! And he was. It was heartbreaking." She paused, recapturing the scene, then continued, "I don't know that I could have done anything more than we had done for him, even if I'd had him in my own bedroom. This little boy had *kwashiorkor*."

It was not refugee camp clinics that had beckoned this nurse to Cambodia after five years in Laos. With Dr. and Mrs. Dean Kroh she had been invited to be in on the beginnings of a hospital in Phnom Penh, to be built by World Vision and staffed by the C & MA, of which all three were a part. When in the course of planning, the decision was made that it would be a pediatrics hospital, Mary Lou was overjoyed, for her speciality is pediatrics. She is a Pediatric Nurse Associate. This extra training was taken for meeting the needs of children in Laos. However, things were shaping up in Cambodia, and it became evident that the greatest need in hospitals there was one for children.

"With great delight," she shared, "we took the plans and adapted them for children's wards. Big sunny wards, pink tile and blue tile, some isolation rooms—" she was obviously reliving happy days of anticipating working in that ideal setting. "I got to oversee everything from the right kinds of sinks for bathing babies, the size the cribs should be and all." A shadow came over her pretty face. "It was real hard to walk off and leave all that when the children so desperately needed it."

Training a corps of Cambodian nurses was another part of the preparation. It was while engaged in such activities awaiting the opening of the hospital that Mary Lou was asked by some of the national Christians if she could send some medicines out to a refugee camp where these Christians were distributing rice and other necessities.

"I don't have anything I could just send with you and say, 'Give one of these to everybody.'" Mary Lou told the men.

"But they need medicine," they insisted.

"So that's how the clinics started in the camps. Actually, Dr. and Mrs. Kroh and I were the first to do this," Mary Lou said with a bright smile. She herself went with quantities of medicine intending to discuss with the camp nurse how they should be administered. But a search revealed there was no camp nurse (some government camps do have one).

She was still thinking about that when people realized that what she had was medicine and they began to swarm and pile all over her, crying, "I'm sick. My baby is sick," and they plopped the little skeletons of kids on her lap.

"Do something for my baby," was the heart-tugging plea.

And she did.

"They all had runny eyes, horrid runny eyes," Mary Lou recalls. "I had eye medicine, but just one tube. I'll never forget how they stood in line, little kids holding their eyes open for me to put the medicine in. Tiny kids—the kind you normally have to fight with to try to get the ointment in—were holding their eyes open, begging 'Me too, me too.'"

The only way she got out that day was by saying, "I'll come back; I promise you I will come back. And I'll bring a doctor and more medicine with me."

The following day, with Dr. and Mrs. Kroh, she did go back, so that they could assess what they could do in the camp. Again they were mobbed by sick people. Disregarding the lack of facilities, they set up shop, sitting on the edge of a porch with pigs running around under their feet.

For Dr. Kroh and his wife, primitive conditions for practicing medicine was no new thing.

"We have been medical missionaries now for over twenty years," he states, "first in Africa (Congo, now called Zaire), now in Cambodia. I remember especially when we were just beginning our careers in Africa. Our equipment was meagre, the facilities primitive. This, combined with our ineptitude in the situation, made me fear the patients would die, so I'd find myself asking the Lord to perform miracles and he would say, 'Operate.' As we did, we just knew the Lord was with us, and the patient would get better. It was a marvelous opportunity to share Christ's love, and many of these patients came to a saving knowledge of Christ through the ministry of the chaplain. I don't believe you can say you are winning souls to the Lord without giving them the Word of God. A medical ministry by itself does not save souls. It takes the Word of God to bring about the new birth and eventual growth in Christ. But we believe that God does use the medical work to open these hearts. We have seen this many, many times. People have come hard of heart, indifferent, and compassion has softened the heart and conditioned the soil for God's Word to be implanted. As Dr. Mooneyham puts it, 'If we are not there when the people need us, why should we expect them to welcome us later?'

"So, as it was in the early days in Africa, conditions in the Cambodia refugee camps were not ideal for medical work."

"It was not unusual," adds Mary Lou, "to hear Esther call out to her husband, 'Dean, Dean! Get that pig away from me' or 'There's a pig after me again, Dean. Do something!' and the doctor would interrupt what he was doing to chase the pigs away from us."

Referring to Dr. Dean Kroh, a village leader said to Stan Mooneyham, "He comes out here and distributes the *Lord*."

"It was as beautiful an expression as I have ever heard," commented Dr. Mooneyham.

The name "Dean" calls to mind another, John Gunther Dean, American ambassador to Cambodia. In addition to his great contribution, his wife showed much compassion for the people, especially the refugees. "Mrs. Dean often worked right alongside us," said Nurse Barbara Neath. "She's a very lovely lady."

Medicine for the clinics was plentifully supplied by World Vision. In fact, World Vision's contribution through medicine, the nutrition centers for

malnourished children operated by them, and their
total efforts to meet raw human need made a
tremendous impact. When the clinics had been
operating for some time, Dr. Stan Mooneyham was
speaking at a meeting and the head man of the camp
showed up and said, "My whole camp would like to
become Christians. No one has ever shown any care
for us like the folk who come to our camp to help
our sick people. We would like to become
Christians," he repeated.

A World Vision photographer offered to help the
people get a church building at the camp. "His name
is David," said Mary Lou, "and since he gave the
hundred dollars to build the bamboo and thatch
structure, we called it St. David's Cathedral! During
the week it's a school, on Sunday it's a church, and
on Thursday school closes and it becomes a clinic.
Sometime later we took David himself to the camp.
The first time he had seen it, the camp was engulfed
in black despair, full of hopeless, sick people. This
time we arrived on a school day and the children were
saying their letters. They were spirited—the whole
atmosphere of the camp was hope. It was beautiful,
and this guy just stood there and cried. I introduced
him and told the people that he was the man who
gave the money for the building. They clapped and
clapped."

With the clinic building available, order was
instituted—patient records, etc. Also, the team
branched out to do the same in other camps.
(Interestingly, some of the secular relief agencies who
had given the missionaries some static—"That's no
way to run a clinic; you can't practice medicine like
that—" began to emulate them, finding it was the
only way to get the job done.) As I listened to Mary
Lou casually share this, I couldn't help thinking of

something Dr. Donald McGavran said at Lausanne: "Bible-taught Christians have always been the world's great achievers."

The perpetual trauma for the medical team was that they could never see all the patients waiting for them in the camps. The people arrived early, before the truck with the team and the medicine, and many of them had walked long miles, having heard that it was clinic day in the camp.

Said Dr. Folkstad, "I just kind of walked around shell-shocked for the first day or so, going into the clinics and finding literally hundreds of mothers and children. Kids were so malnourished, dying of diseases not even being treated by any doctor.

"The hardest thing I ever did," he recalled with deep feeling, "was triage (selecting according to greatest need the patients who would be seen that day—and those who would not). The first time I did it, I came back into the clinic and it just wrecked the entire day for me! Here were between 500 and 700, and I had to go out and pick 150–200 of them, and send the rest away: 'I'm sorry but we can't see you today.'"

"It's the most heartrending thing we have to do," Mary Lou agrees. "Mothers saying, 'My baby, too,' 'My baby is convulsing,' 'My baby has fever'; and they're all pulling at you, begging to be next, just asking a chance for life for their child! We used to hand them cards with a number, then we found that some were selling the numbers because it would give them a little bit of money for food. So we took a felt pen and marked the number on the child's hand."

Dr. Penelope Key (Dr. Penny to her colleagues), the director of World Vision medical team in Cambodia, wrote out of her own struggle:

I waved good-bye to a little Cambodian girl leaving her native country for her new home and family in America. Beside me, my Cambodian doctor colleague said, "She is a lucky, lucky little girl. Why did she get chosen?"

Today, in my clinic at the Cambodian refugee center, there were more than 500 mothers with their sick children, waiting their turn. Some will come again tomorrow, and some the next day. I chose the 200 to 300 children from among them. The rest are the unchosen.

There is agony for me in this choosing. When I put up my hand to my doctors, nurses and clerks, "That child is the last one for the morning," what am I doing or saying to the child *after* the last one? The anguish of the mother whose child is refused haunts me and my staff. Her face stays with us as we eat our lunch, knowing that she is waiting and watching her child.

Sometimes a waiting child dies while I am away resting. How then can I rest, or eat, or sleep? How can I not choose to see that child? Why did I choose to stop at the child before that one? If I had chosen to see one more child, that child might be alive today.

This morning there were thirty-four children needing admission to the hospital. There were only seven empty cots. I had to choose. Twenty-seven critically ill children went to their homes in the arms of their despairing mothers . . .

All these children are God's little ones. He loves and cares about every one of them. I believe he wants every one of them to be cared

for. He does not want me to choose one from
another. He loves them all.

I have a prayer I use:

"Lord, don't let me have to go on choosing
which child. Lord, send me more doctors.
Lord, send me more cots, more hospitals,
more medicines, milk and food. Lord, give all
these children enough food so they won't get
sick. Lord, please stop this senseless war."

Becca was one chosen from a line of sick
children in my clinic. Did I choose her? Did
God choose her? Or is she just an exceedingly
fortunate little girl? When can all my children be
chosen for a new, happy life?[1]

(David Aikman, *Time* correspondent, describes Dr.
Penelope Key as "a veteran of medical work in New
Guinea" and quotes her as saying, "I grew tired of
pulling arrows out of tribesmen.")

Another area of frustration for the doctors in the
refugee camps was the difficulty in getting a medical
history. Says Dr. Kroh, "We would ask, 'Where is
your husband, or your father?' and the answer so
often would be, 'He was killed by the V.C.' (Viet
Cong); they used this term loosely. One morning I
was examining a child of about nine months. His
sister was holding him; he'd just gotten over measles
and he had full-blown pneumonia. We gave him some
penicillin and some other medication and asked where
the parents were. This was a time when the Khmer
Rouge had overrun a section about eight miles
outside Phnom Penh. The father and mother were
killed, but somehow the seven children had been able
to escape and were living in a temple area in the city.
It just seemed so overwhelming to wonder how they

[1] *World Vision*, April 1975, p. 9.

were going to manage. The distribution of food isn't all that regular. We gave them milk, and they were going back to the temple area.

"Another instance of the difficulty of obtaining any history: A woman came with her child. They were both so painfully skinny. She sat down in front of us and we asked her history but she couldn't even talk; she was just overcome by grief. They're not people who cry out loud, but between her tears she tried to tell us. Her husband and two other children had been killed instantly when a rocket slammed into their small home. She had lost an eye through shrapnel. She and the baby had come to this camp with nothing, just the clothes on their back—no mats, no cooking pots, no money. We called one of the laymen who had begun to minister at this camp (he himself had just been saved three or four months), and he went with this mother and our missionary nurse and inspected her quarters to see what they could do for her. They supplied her with what she needed and just before they left, this Christian Cambodian brother talked to her about the love of Jesus, that he loved her and wanted to help her. So each week she came for medication, for milk, and whatever we might have in the way of protein food.

"Even in the midst of the heartache there was the positive side. As they have heard the gospel, it has brought great joy and consolation to know that Jesus is there to help them. We had a baby die right on our patio, and because of our inability really to speak the language well, my wife invited the mother to come to church the next Sunday. We had told the pastor about the death of this child, but he didn't know that the mother was in the service that morning. However, he gave a beautiful message on death and heaven. This woman listened as he spoke about babies being in heaven, and she could hardly wait until the end of the service so that she could accept the Lord. And now, because of her own assurance and the joy in her heart, she has opened her little home and about twenty people are coming each Sunday for a service. This is one of four such meetings in that camp.

"Some might think that our going to Cambodia was two and a half years wasted, because the hospital—the reason for our going—was never opened. But we don't feel it was a waste, because our investment was in the souls of men. We were out in the refugee camps ministering to the people physically, in the name of Jesus, and we had the privilege of opening our home for a Sunday service. We invited a national pastor to do the preaching and, starting with twenty or so, we've seen a real harvest. All told, in the four services held in this camp, hundreds have come to Christ. So our hearts are thrilled that this opportunity was ours."

One of the diseases the medical team was not prepared for was *kwashiorkor* (protein deficiency which in its severest form produces heart failure). Once the body is depleted of protein, the heart muscle begins to deteriorate and then the heart is not able to eliminate fluid. The patient gets edema; the skin breaks down. They appear to have burns.

Nurse Mary Lou recalls the first case she saw.

"I remember quizzing a mother; I was sure her child had been burned, but she kept saying it hadn't. It took us quite a while to realize that we were dealing with *kwashiorkor*. When a French-Cambodian nurse friend of mine heard us talking about *kwashiorkor*, she said the Cambodian word for it, then told us it translates literally, 'the child off the breast.' And this is the problem in these countries—as long as the child is breastfeeding, he is getting protein (that

is, if the mother is being fed herself); when he no
longers gets breast milk, if he does not get enough
other milk, he can develop *kwashiorkor*. Normally, (in
Africa, for instance, where it was first diagnosed)
kwashiorkor is found in the child who is suddenly
weaned with no milk to replace his mother's. But in
Cambodia, we saw this in a wide variety of children;
from tiny babies to ten-year-olds.

"I thought, *Why have I not seen this in Laos? They
have refugees, they've had war longer than Cambodia.*
Then it came to me that Laos has many tribal people,
mountain people; they know every leaf in the forest;
they know roots that sustain life. And they know how
to eat lizards, even rats and mice, anything that will
provide protein."

[Author's note: I can add my eyewitness
documentation of what Mary Lou describes. I had the
privilege of visiting in a tribal village—the village of
the Kapok Tree—in Laos, and one of the first to greet
me was a smiling little girl, maybe eight years old,
dangling a string of crickets she had caught and
which, I was told, she would roast over the fire and
eat.

Cambodians have, however, been the best fed
people in all that region, so theirs is a very different
situation from Laos. Cambodians are, in a sense,
suddenly starving; it's been a very drastic change.]

"I could tell story after story of starving orphans,"
says Mary Lou, "children whose mothers had been
killed in rocket attacks, and nobody in the family
knew how to artificially feed a baby. One that sticks
in my mind is a little boy I called 'the little sparrow,'
for that's what he reminded me of. He was perhaps a
year old. His mother had died of typhoid and his
father was out fighting; a twelve-year-old sister was
left to care for him. He showed up in the clinic

obviously malnourished. The little girl's reason for bringing him to us was that he hadn't been sleeping.

"She asked, 'Will you look at my baby brother? He can't sleep at night. He cries all night.' As we got the history, we realized the child was starving. We got him over to the nutrition center, and he kept his little mouth open as long as we would poke something into it, just like a baby bird! So we fed him through the day and his sister took him home. The next day as we drove up, there was a bright-eyed, smiling little girl holding her baby brother. She said, 'My aunt wants to know what kind of medicine you gave my baby brother. He slept all night and he has never slept all night since my mother died.' I said, 'We didn't give him any medicine; we gave him food.' All they had been giving that baby was a little rice water; they didn't know, they just didn't realize what food they could give a baby, even just mashing up a banana, for example. They do know about milk, but they use sweetened condensed milk which has so much sugar in proportion to milk that a child couldn't possibly take enough of it to supply the needed protein. And unless the protein deficiency can be reversed in time, *kwashiorkor* is certain to result.

"I found myself telling a mother, 'This child needs some food; be sure to give him some fish and other good foods he can handle.' A couple of mothers glared at me with hate in their eyes for making such a suggestion. One said, 'How am I going to feed my baby fish; I have no fish.' I said, 'How about an egg?' and got the same response, so we realized we had to do something about it. We could clear up a child's pneumonia, but then we would have a malnourished child who wouldn't get well. This was when we launched the eight-hour daily nutrition camps. And it was from there I had to drive out at sundown one day knowing that my favorite little boy would be dead by morning.

"This child was special to me because of his big sister. Their father was a soldier and the mother, who had tuberculosis, was gone all day working as a scrub woman. The children were ten, five, and three years old. The ten-year-old girl was so bright and pretty, and she came faithfully every week, just trying to have the little ones checked and to get some food for them. We all loved her so much. The children were terribly malnourished. We did everything we could, but it was her brother that died. And, oh, I wished it had been my own brother!

"We had two others die shortly after, and I was just ready to give up. I was in the car with Dr. Penny Key, an Australian doctor. She was my referral on all this nutrition thing; I was kind of on loan for this project, working under Dr. Key.

" 'Penny,' I admitted to her, 'I just can't go on any more,' and she very firmly answered, 'Mary Lou, what is the mortality rate of *kwashiorkor* untreated?'

" 'Well, untreated it's 100 percent,' I replied. 'Right. Treated in the finest institutions, it is 50 percent,' she reminded me. 'We have lost three, and we have pulled through twenty. We're doing all right!'

"Knowing that, I could keep on. We have lost them, and it's hard. But I can drive into that camp and see little kids come bouncing out to meet the car and know what they used to be, know that we did pull them through when there was no hope.

"We see mothers when their child has begun to smile again. It's a great thing when a child begins to smile.

"There is the heartbreak of *kwashiorkor*. But there are the triumphs also! There are the nurses who cared.

"Whatever happens to our beautiful new hospital, we have the satisfaction of knowing that we left behind, besides tiles and plaster, twenty-one nurses who cared what happened to the sick little babies and the children."

Hoping to have all Christian personnel to staff the children's hospital, under the direction of Dr. Kroh a program was begun to train national nurses. These were recruited through the ranks of the church, high school graduates who expressed a desire to be nurses. Facilities, equipment, and a place for training made it impossible for a regular nurses' program to be carried on. The emphasis was on pediatrics. A Practical Nurses' course was simplified for the twenty-one fellows and girls, and classes were held for three hours a day, five days a week. Those speaking faltering English when the school started showed tremendous interest and improved rapidly in the language. All twenty-one students came faithfully every day. Some worked at their job until 1:00 or 1:30, but they were right there for the start of class at 2:00. A number of them had to walk long distances, but they never missed.

Five nurses shared the instruction: Esther Kroh, Mary Lou Rorabaugh, Barbara Neath, Lynn Walsh, and Carol Weston.

"I enjoyed seeing the students change," shares Mary Lou, "from the typical national attitude, 'Now I'm going to be a nurse; I'll just sit there and supervise or something like that.' Rather, they began to see the real challenge in caring for children. By their own responses we could tell that we were instilling in this group of students the idea of more than giving a child an injection if someone would pay them a bribe. They began to watch the child and want to help to make him well and healthy and happy. At first they were amazed that it was important to keep a child happy. This was all something new to them and they latched right on to it. They even started to suggest ways and means they could accomplish this. For instance, a child's fears: How do you keep a child from being afraid? And they were giving us suggestions from their culture which were extremely good.''

To be sure, at the beginning of the program, they didn't like the idea of having a lot of work to do! When the nurses said that babies must be checked at least every hour, one boy raised his hand and said, ''But when are we going to sleep?''

''Well,'' the instructor answered, ''some will work only at night and they will sleep in the daytime.''

''Sleep in the daytime!'' The students sounded incredulous. They resisted the whole ''foolish idea,'' but bit by bit it became a most important concept. They were going to watch those babies, they were going to make sure nothing happened to one of them if right nursing could help! It became all-important to these students that each baby was able to breathe easily, that they weren't going to choke with mucus in their throat, etc.

Opportunities for practical experience were not as available as the teachers would have liked; they had planned an additional twenty hours beyond what was actually given. But, observing and listening as the students were doing some practical work in a children's facility, the missionary instructors were more than repaid with the attitudes of this group of young Cambodian Christian nursing students.

Said Mary Lou, ''They noticed a nurse just sitting doing nothing while the baby she was in charge of obviously needed her attention. They were incensed at her indifference. Then they saw a nurse just dump some medicine down a baby's throat. The child choked and gagged and the nurse went on her way to another patient. Our nurses just looked at me with horror, then exclaimed, '*She's not doing that right*! She's supposed to *hold* that baby.' You could just feel their involvement and concern as they kept saying, 'If a baby begins to choke, you should help it to breathe before you give it any more.' 'And if it spits it up, she's supposed to repeat the medicine.'

"It was such a delight to us that these lessons had really gotten across, that *caring* is such a big part of nursing.

" 'You are exactly right,' we assured our students, 'and we are very proud of you.'

"They completed their training and wrote their final exams. We held a graduation ceremony for them in the lovely new Children's Hospital: the first corps of Cambodian Christian nurses (granted, it was an abbreviated course). And the very next day we had to leave."

Heartbreak, yes. But there were the triumphs.

The *new* nurses did not have to leave.

9

Something More Than Buddhism

In a country where changing one's religion was tantamount to betraying his citizenship, there would have to be strong motivation for such a reversal on the part of an individual. How significant then is this report in *World Vision* magazine:

> Of the 1,011 inquirers who filled out decision forms at the New Life Crusade held by Dr. Stan Mooneyham in April 1972, many specifically mentioned that they were "seeking something more than Buddhism." More than 90 percent of these were young men between eighteen and thirty.[1]

Up to 1970, Cambodia was one of the strongest

---

[1]Billy Bray, "The Church That Multiplied Nearly Three Times," *World Vision*, May 1972, p. 6.

Buddhist countries in Asia. Every village had its
Buddhist temple; 85,000 priests were a constant
reminder of the national religion. But with the
outbreak of war, the people were violently uprooted.
They saw the destruction of their temples—much
more significant to them than losing our church
buildings would be to most of us. The temple was the
hub of life, both social and educational (schools were
on the temple grounds). Even the political influence
came from the temple.

Asked "Why did you become a Christian instead of
remaining a Buddhist?" Rev. Ching Ching Wang,
formerly of Hong Kong and now of San Francisco,
replied, "Buddhism is good. But judged by Christian
standards, it is not good enough."

Without exception, every person I interviewed as
to the possible explanation of the spiritual
phenomenon in Cambodia was unanimous on this one
point—disillusionment with their own religion; the
failure of the Buddhist religion in a time of severe,
desperate need.

It's interesting then to follow this stream of thought
as it leads us to the ultimate reason why the gospel
found little or no foothold in this land for half a
century of good missionaries who appear to have
known what they were doing; they had their priorities
straight; discouragement did not daunt them; they
kept believing God had sent them there, even though
through the years the government would not
recognize them as a church. Why? Because Cambodia
is a strongly Buddhist country. They had not changed
their corporate religious mind one little bit from the
day when they decreed, "There is no place in
Cambodia for Christian missionaries."

As Tom Wisley pointed out to me, the Buddhist
religion in Cambodia has not been watered down by

animist beliefs, as has happened in Viet Nam and
Laos. Animism is there in Cambodia, but it doesn't
have a hold on people; you don't, for instance, see
them with the spirit strings to ward off evil, strings
that have been blessed by the animist priests.*

I had seen those spirit strings tied around wrists in
neighboring Laos. At the airport, for example, I
noticed some Lao people ceremoniously tying a string
around the wrist of a passenger they were seeing off
(in the way we sometimes pin a corsage). Curious, I
questioned my missionary escort, Mrs. Helen Sawyer,
as we boarded the plane together.

She explained that the string had been blessed and
was tied on the person to keep him from danger and
evil on his journey. (As that old DC-3 rocked and
rolled and jostled us about, I began to think they had
a point.)

By contrast with Laos, *on the surface,* Buddhism,
unadulterated with animistic superstition (except
possibly in the tribal villages), has traditionally met
the people's needs. This is in contrast to what the
Right Hon. Malcolm McDonald wrote:

> The religion which they were forced to
> acknowledge never really commanded their deep
> spiritual allegiance. The common Khmer people,
> like most Asian peasantry, had always remained
> animist at heart, worshiping the spirits of woods
> and rivers and fields.[2]

Nevertheless, the monks, the priests, the
pagodas—these had filled their life. They lived by
their doctrine of cause and effect (*karma*) which says
in essence, "If you do evil in this present life, it will

*Some missionaries debate Mr. Wisley's theory; they claim that
Cambodian Buddhism *is* tainted with animism.
[2]*Angkor,* n.p.

mean suffering in the next incarnation."

This doctrine also helps people to endure stress.

Again quoting Mr. Wisley, "If you have a lot of bad *karma,* then a lot of bad things are going to happen to you; if you have good *karma,* then good things happen to you—a cardinal teaching in Buddhism. (This is highly simplified: it really is more sophisticated than the way I've stated it. But very briefly that is the way it is.) So that when these people, a whole nation (11 million people) began to see that everybody was having 'bad luck,' as they call it, which of course resulted from the amount of bad *karma* they had, they began to ask themselves very logical, practical questions, such as: Are we all this bad? Do we all have this much bad *karma?* I think this is just one factor that has caused a sense of religious frustration, developed a religious vacuum within the people. This is a serious area because religion in any culture, especially in agrarian cultures, is always a big thing.

"Another thing that has to do with it is this: A woman is standing in the market buying something. Her children are with her, maybe her husband is beside her. A rocket lands within fifteen feet. Her husband is killed, her children are maimed, and she is standing there holding a bleeding baby; the child is dying in her arms and Buddhism can only say 'This is a result of your bad *karma.*' There is no real area of comfort for this woman; and this happens again and again and again, and people, even if they are not highly educated, can at least ask themselves these basic questions. So this has developed a religious vacuum where the people didn't really have anything they could hang onto, or believe in anyone. They could no longer believe in Sihanouk, whom they had believed in strongly. He fled the country."

As a refugee explained to me, "We had no king."

Esther Kroh shared with me her thoughtful evaluation of the situation. "I think a big factor is just the general spirit of young people being tired of what is happening in the country. It really all goes back to the war, but it's the idea that for years they have just lived by their Buddhist principles and never really thought much for themselves.

"As is true all over the world, young people in Cambodia are becoming aware that they can have ideas and do things differently from their parents. Before, years ago, they would have been afraid of the impact in their home if they accepted something different, but now they don't seem to be afraid of what their parents would do, and they are willing to step out on this. It seems as soon as they get a little bit of knowledge of the Bible, that the Lord just enlightens them so, and they realize how wonderful it is. Some of them out in the provinces have only heard over the radio, yet they were writing in saying, 'I want to know more about this wonderful Christian life. I want to live a pure life. Tell me how I can live a pure life.' It just seems the Lord opens up their minds, they would just hear a little bit and yet they were hungry for more. I think it's just the spirit of the age and dissatisfaction with Buddhism."

Mr. Ci Thai Sing, director of the National Museum and one of the many government officials who came to Christ, said that he believes the older generation is tied to Buddhism but that younger Cambodians "have abandoned the temples and no longer believe in Buddhism."[3]

On October 9, 1970, Cambodia became a republic. This brought great hope to the people. But they

[3] *World Vision*, May 1972.

almost immediately found themselves in a war for which they were not prepared; they were unarmed; they were not interested in fighting. As this war dragged on, there was little prosperity, and conditions deteriorated. People became disillusioned by the corruption that went disregarded and unchecked by the officials.

So the educated began to leave the country, creating a brain drain to France.

"With rockets and frightening news day after day, we began to see the people with their guard down," says Gene Hall. He explains, "When formerly in my English classes, I would talk about Jesus, they would turn me off. But when bad news came, how they would soak it in. High officials listened to the gospel, for these were times that tried men's souls."

"We've had five years of war in Cambodia," comments Norman Ens, "and it just seems as though this has really shaken them and they realize that their dependence upon Buddhism just left them in a big void. This opened them up to ponder that there must be something else that would satisfy them; so this heart hunger is a very definite factor. Also, when people are desperate, when they're sad, when as it has been in Cambodia, almost every family has been directly involved in death, somebody in the family has died, and when they turn to Buddhism to find comfort, of course there is none. And those who have turned to the Lord see that there *is* comfort in Jesus Christ, so immediately they tell their families and friends, and it just snowballs."

With her warm smile, Marie took up the narrative as we sat in my hotel room in Vientiane, Laos, in March 1975. "The Lord has really done very wonderful things to prove himself to people when they've trusted him. Or even before they knew

enough to know how to trust him, he has proven that
he is worthy of their trust. There was one woman
who used to go every single day to sell fish; every day
in the month she'd go and sit in the same place and
sell fish. She had been witnessed to. She was thinking
of trusting the Lord, but she wasn't quite sure yet.
She still had some question in her mind whether this
was all true or not. And then one day, she thought,
'Well, I guess today I won't go and sell fish.' No
particular reason. She just thought she'd stay home.
That day a rocket landed exactly where she would
have been sitting. People were killed; she would have
most certainly been killed if she had gone out that
day. She immediately recognized that *Jesus in whom she
had not yet put her trust* had protected her. She
couldn't wait then to come over to the house and give
her heart to the Lord. When she came, she just
beamed and beamed and said, 'Oh, it's true. I really
believe it. I really believe it. He protected me. It's
really true.'"

It seemed that many times the Lord would do
things for them in a very tangible, definite way so that
they would understand that he is real. And if all
they're trusting Jesus for is eternal life, that doesn't
help them very much for today. They need something
to prove he will help them for today too.

And God beautifully met this need. He gave them
something more than Buddhism.

As the desperate people arrived in new places
where there were only strangers, the Christians began
to have an influence in small but real ways; they
showed Christian love to the people. This accelerated
over the years, especially as the situation in Cambodia
became more and more critical. The Christians have
had a useful ministry, showing love in a tangible way,
as James exhorts. And what about Jesus himself, who

taught us that if a man has two coats and another has none, we should give him one?

Christian compassion has made an impact. By contrast, the Buddhist priest begs daily, even from the refugees, stricken and impoverished though they are. (In Bangkok, a Buddhist young person explained to me that the priests' begging is really an opportunity for people to gain merit by giving something for the begging bowls.) It was the Christians who helped to relieve the misery of the refugees and meet their bodily needs. Christians were the first medical teams to minister to the sick in the camps. They had something better than Buddhism.

How can we contrast what Christ has to offer to those who put their trust in him, and what Buddhism offers?

Mr. Wang, knowing Buddhism thoroughly, repudiated this religion in favor of accepting Christ. He formerly taught Chinese religions at the Lutheran Bible Institute in Hong Kong. "I would have been a Buddhist priest today," he declares, "if I had not met Christ. Why then did I become a Christian?" Wang has written about his ten reasons for the change:

1. Buddhism is polytheistic or atheistic.
   Christianity believes in one supreme God.
   Every religion has some kind of faith, even the most primitive religions. The important question is not whether or not you are sincere in your faith. The important question is *what* you believe. If what you believe is false, your thinking, behavior, and enjoyments, which combine together to form your entire life, will proceed in a certain direction. If what you believe is true, then your life will proceed in a quite different direction. Hence, a person must

take care to determine whether a religion is false
or true in its teachings and make a choice
accordingly.

We see Buddhists devoutly worshiping their
gods, but unfortunately none of those gods is the
true God. Recently a so-called "new Buddhism"
seems to be arising. They worship only a few
images, such as Gautama Buddha, Amitaba
Buddha, and the goddess of Mercy (Kuan-yin).
But these gods are still not the true God.

Many Buddhists mistakenly think that the God
of Christianity is one of their several Buddhist
gods, and that the Christian heaven is merely
one among their many unstable Buddhist
heavens. This misunderstanding is intentional in
order that they may proudly say that Buddhism
is superior to Christianity. I have often met
people who think in this way.

The most important god in Buddhism should
be Gautama. Yet Gautama himself was not God.
He never commanded men to worship him as
God. According to the Buddha nature, the
Buddhas and all living creatures are on the same
level. All human beings can become Buddhas if
they attain enlightenment. In Buddhism there is
no concept of a personal God whom man must
worship.

That is why a Buddhist patriarch once split a
wooden Buddha image in two and burnt it.
Because he could not find the supreme God, he
believed that he himself was the highest one in
the universe. Alas! He did not know that he
himself was an insignificant, inferior, and weak
being, not at all mighty.

Christianity has a strikingly different concept
of God. In many ways God spoke to men of old

by the prophets. Although the prophets' message is limited and man's comprehension is sometimes deep and at other times shallow, in these last days he has spoken to us by his only Son Jesus Christ (Hebrews 1:1). The one true God is Jehovah. He is not only the Truth (John 18:37), the Word (*logos*) of the beginning (John 1:1), the "I-am-who-I-am" (Exodus 3:14), he is also the supreme God who has almighty power, wisdom, love, holiness, righteousness, and a living personality (Isaiah 45:18; Genesis 17:1; Psalm 147:5; John 17:3). He is the only true God whom human beings ought to worship.

2. Buddhism views this world not as created by God, but as having four distinct elements; namely, earth, water, fire, and wind, linked together by *Hepuprataya,* or primary and secondary causes, without any plan and purpose. Christianity views the world as created by God according to his own design and purpose.

Buddhist friends can not see the beauty of the world and the grace of God's creation if they merely follow Buddha's teaching. They see this world as one full of misery, and everything in it as vanity. The world is not from God, but is the result of *karma,* the law of cause and effect.

The Christian view is quite the opposite. We believe this natural world is created by God, and that it is great and wonderful. Rich treasures are hidden which man can use for abundant living. In many kinds of plants, flowers, birds, animals, minerals, music, and arts, we can discern the boundless universe and the invisible atom. These things can all be used to benefit mankind. If our spiritual eyes are open, we can discern the boundless universe and the invisible

boundless universe and the invisible
atom—everywhere we can see the wonderful,
mysterious creation of God (Psalm 19).

3. The Buddhist view of life is one of pessimism.
   The Christian view of life is one of optimism.
   Buddhist friends may not admit that they are
pessimistic, but Buddhism views life as distress.
There are eight kinds of distress: birth, old age,
sickness, death, parting with what we love,
meeting with what we hate, unattained aims, and
all the ills of the five *skandhas* (aggregates). A
human being is destined to suffer, according to
Buddhism. But Christians are optimistic. They
are willing to serve family, society, nation, and
the world at large. They feel that the more they
serve, the more they can glorify God.

4. Buddhism is an attempt to escape from the
   world;
   Christianity seeks participation in the affairs of
   the world.
   Why did Gautama Buddha become a monk?
Because he saw the misery of birth, old age,
sickness, and death. Such things made him give
up human love and leave his old father, young
wife, and newborn son. Later on, this influenced
his wife and son, aunt, cousins, and other
relatives as well as many maid-servants to
become monks and nuns. Why did they choose
such a life? Because such is Buddhist teaching.
Although in Mahayana Buddhism the
Boddhissattva can have a temporary family,
marriage is still the source of *karma,* the source
of all distresses.
   Christianity on the contrary, recognizes that
marriage is God's plan and that a family is a gift

of God. In chapter 19 of Matthew, Jesus said,
"Have you not read that he who made them
from the beginning made them male and female,
and said for this reason a man shall leave his
father and mother and be joined to his wife, and
the two shall become one"? Christians need not
leave their parents, wife, children, and relatives
in order to be obedient children of God in this
world. When we pass away from this world, we
go to live with God, our heavenly Father. Here
is how Jesus prayed: "I'm not asking you to take
them out of the world, but to keep them safe
from Satan's power" (John 17:15).

5. Buddhism is fatalistic in its beliefs.
   Christianity believes in the will of God.
   Buddhists believe that riches, poverty,
blessings, distresses, short or long life in this
world are all caused by *karma* from past lives.
This doctrine began with Gautama Buddha.
When Gautama was ill with food poisoning, he
told his disciples that it was due to the *karma*
from a previous life, because he had knowingly
given the wrong medicine to a patient. Therefore
he had to suffer food poisoning in his present
life. When an army from the north came to
destroy Gautama's race, he said that this was also
karma from a past life; this calamity could not be
avoided, because for a long period in the past,
the northern soldiers were fish in a pool and
were eaten by Gautama's race. Such was
Gautama's understanding of the danger to his
race and country. Therefore he did not go to
save his country.
   By contrast, Christians do not believe in
karma. Instead, they seek to know the will of

God in every situation and act accordingly.

Christian life is like this because Jesus Christ's life was like this. Once Jesus passed by a man blind at birth and his disciples asked him, "Master, who did sin, this man, or his parents, that he was born blind?" Jesus did not say this man had sinned or his parents had sinned. He said instead that now the works of God might be made manifest in him, because Jesus would cure his blind eyes. Jesus knew that time was short, that he had to work while it was day. Night would come, when no one can work (John 9).

One day I talked with a Buddhist who said, "We have no *Pratyaya,* that is, no *karma* connection, so we had better not talk to each other." I replied, "I don't care about *karma* connection; I know it is God's will that I should talk with everyone whenever I have the opportunity to do so" (Matthew 26:39; Romans 12:2).

6. Buddhism declares that all creatures have the Buddha nature and are of equal rank.
   Christianity declares that men are superior to other creatures.

The Buddhist term "sattya" means "all living creatures." These are differentiated by four forms of birth, namely, womb birth (such as men or other animals); egg birth (such as birds); moisture or water birth (such as mosquitoes or fish); metamorphic birth (such as worms and butterflies). Buddhism also claims that all living creatures must pass through six stages of Transmigration. Therefore, Buddhists dare not eat pork, beef, chicken, and fish. If they do, they might eat their parents or grandparents or other relatives.

Although they cannot recognize such animals as the reincarnation of their ancestors, they still dare not eat meat, because every creature's Buddha-nature is equal. If you eat a chicken, you will be reborn a chicken to be eaten by the one whom you have eaten in order to compensate life. This is *karma,* which nobody can break. That is why Buddhists buy fish and set them free in a river, or buy pigs and oxen to feed in a Buddhist temple.

Christians know there is a difference between men and animals. When God created all things, man alone was created in his image. This image is spiritual, not physical. The Apostle Paul said, "And have put on the new nature, which is being renewed in knowledge after the image of its creator" (Colossians 3:10, RSV; also see Ephesians 4:24).

Buddhists always criticize the "narrow love" of Christians who only love human beings and do not love animals. Buddhist monks and nuns on the contrary are concerned about loving animals, not about loving their families.

7. Buddhism urges people to believe in Buddha in order to escape suffering and secure happiness.
   Christianity urges people to believe in Jesus in order to be redeemed from sin and be saved.

A Buddhist leaves home to become a monk or a vegetarian and chant Buddha's name in order to accumulate merit for his next birth, and to acquire happiness. He pays no attention to sin; his sole aim is to escape sufferings. Christianity gives first attention to sin, not to suffering. A

Christian is bidden to carry his cross, to follow Jesus in the midst of family and society. "No cross, no crown." But he hates sins as a great enemy.

8. A Buddhist tries to work out his own salvation by keeping the Buddhist commandments. A Christian receives salvation of God as a free gift of grace.

This is the greatest difference between these two religions. Before Gautama Buddha died, his disciples cried and said, "Master, who will be our master after your death?" Gautama said, "*Pratimoksa* will be your master instead of me." *Pratimoksa* means the commandments. Buddhists have many methods of self-culture, but even for "Pure Land" Buddhists who express faith in Buddha Amitaba, the first step is to keep the commandments. Gautama never said, "I can save you" or "I shall forgive your sins."

A Christian knows that man cannot save himself by keeping laws. St. Paul said, "For no human being will be justified in his sight by works of the law, since through the law comes knowledge of sin . . . the righteousness of God through faith in Jesus Christ for all who believe . . . They are justified by his grace as a gift, through the redemption which is in Christ Jesus, whom God put forward as an expiation by his blood, to be received by faith" (Romans 3:20–25, RSV). "And you must understand, my brothers, that this is through him, Jesus Christ, that forgiveness of sins is now being proclaimed to you. It is through him that everyone who has faith is acquitted of everything for which there was no acquittal under the law of Moses" (Acts 13:38,39).

9. Buddhist doctrine teaches that man must take
   only vegetarian food.
   Christianity teaches that food is for health and
   does not concern the soul.

When I was a Buddhist, I ate no meat, not
even eggs, because eggs may become chickens.
This was very troublesome for me when I left
home to work in society. I could not board with
my colleagues. I could not join any feast given
by friends. My aunt was a Buddhist, but her
children were not, so their families also had
conflicts over the food problem.

Since becoming a Christian, I am free from
such difficulties. I am at liberty to go to any
restaurant, and to accept my friends' hospitality,
for Christ's teaching is, "Evil words come from
an evil heart, and defile the man who says them.
For from the heart come evil thoughts" (see
Matthew 15:1–20). "Food will not commend us
to God. We are no worse if we do not eat, and
no better off if we do" (1 Corinthians 8:8). "The
important thing for us as Christians is not what we
eat or drink but stirring up goodness and peace
and joy from the Holy Spirit" (Romans 14:17).

10. Buddhism's ultimate goal is Nirvana.
    Christianity's ultimate goal is eternal life.

When Gautama was eighty years old, he
became sick and died under the Bodhi-tree; and
as Buddhists believe, he entered Nirvana. The
goal of every Buddhist is Nirvana which means
"tranquil extinction."

Buddhists have different ideas about the real
state of Nirvana. I have asked several Buddhist
priests, "After one has entered Nirvana, does he
still exist as an individual?" Their answers

varied. Some said the personality remains, and others said that personality is absolutely extinguished. One, for instance, said that if a drop of water falls into the sea, that one drop of water exists no more. Another argued, "Surely you cannot find this single drop of water; the water exists, but individuality disappears."

Christianity gives an assured answer to this question. "For God loved the world so much that he gave his only Son so that anyone who believes in him shall not perish but have eternal life" (John 3:16). Such a life is not physical or carnal desires of flesh; it is spiritual life and comes from God (John 1:12, 13). Such life is not obtained after death but begins in the present world, when man is born again in Jesus (1 John 5:13). Although in the beginning the desires of the flesh are strong and the spiritual life is feeble, this spiritual life knows the Holy Spirit and has communion with God so it becomes abundant (1 Corinthians 2:14).

Such life yields the fruit of the Spirit: "love, joy, peace, patience, kindness, goodness, faithfulness, gentleness, self-control" (Galatians 5:22).

Such life overcomes sin (1 John 3:9; Ephesians 2:1–6).

Such life overcomes sickness, sword, fire, and tribulation (Romans 8:35–37).

Such life overcomes death and the power of the Devil (Matthew 16:18; 1 Corinthians 15:55–57; 2 Timothy 1:10).

Such life is given to man through Jesus. "I have written this to you so that you may know you have eternal life" (1 John 5:13).

Eternal life can be obtained by man in this present time and in this world.

What was the something more than Buddhism could offer?

The indwelling Christ!

Buddhism has, as we've seen, its good behavior code, its "commandments"; but without the ability to observe every rule, to obey and live by its precepts, knowledge of its commandments only imposes a burden of guilt. The individual knows he can never quite measure up. For the Buddhist this is a life quest which is at the same time a dead-end street.

God has so made us that the most primitive dweller in the jungle, the most sophisticated modern in his concrete jungle, the most rigorously dedicated religionist has within him a conscience that will not quit. It blinks "stop" or "go" as we rationalize our behavior. In itself, however, this alter ego has no power, none whatever, to enable us to obey the rules, to measure up totally. Not only Buddhists, but all people have to live with this internal struggle. We know we cannot ever shape up sufficiently—until we meet and accept Jesus Christ who did the shaping up for us.

Jesus is the "something more" that empowers us. He is "something more than Buddha."

"Our god left us a doctrine, but *he died.*"

This was the despair voiced by disillusioned Buddhists as they saw their temples falling, their villages in flames. Especially in the final months, many of them lost all hope. Many said, "We've passed all hope." They felt totally abandoned. No wonder then that when they heard about Jesus, one of the phrases most often on their lips was, "I've found Jesus, the living Christ."

To a man, these Khmer Christians would assert, "We have found something better than Buddhism."

10

Exodus with Unity

On February 23, 1975, Dr. Nathan Bailey, president of the Christian & Missionary Alliance, after carefully evaluating what was happening in and around the city of Phnom Penh, asked all C & MA missionaries to temporarily withdraw from the Khmer Republic.

Since January the Mekong River, the main supply line into the city, had been closed. With rebel forces gradually forming a line around the city, it was felt prudent for the missionary staff to leave.

"When I reported this word to the missionaries," said field chairman Rev. Gene Hall, "some wept. All were shocked. We were very much aware of the seriousness of the situation, but we were equally aware of a mighty moving of God upon the Khmer Republic. The small church which in 1970 had three places of worship in Phnom Penh now had twenty-seven. The tempo of increase had quickened dramatically, especially in 1974. In fact, in just the first six months there were as many new worshipers as there were in the previous *fifty years*!

"When the directive comes to evacuate, the job of the field chairman is to so implement it as to achieve exodus with unity."

Torn up himself at the thought that he must leave, it was still his responsibility to accomplish the smooth transition of all leadership.

An experienced missionary, Mr. Hall is no stranger to evacuation. "The transition to total national responsibility is not performed the day you walk away from the field," Gene philosophized. "Rather it is one of the underlying principles of sound mission work. Actually, for us, transition started back when we returned in 1970. Ten years earlier, in a move to oust all American missionaries, when visas expired, they were not renewed. This was Prince Sihanouk's polite way of saying, 'We don't want you.' As we were gradually phased out, the Khmer church was left without any foreign leadership. When we returned, we did so *at the invitation of the Christians.* And we came back with the determination, 'I've come, Lord Jesus, to be a servant to the national church.' And we endeavored to do this. When, therefore, the time came for us to leave, there was not the need for a frantic running around trying to find someone capable of assuming the leadership. True, there was a vacuum in the supplementary ministries of training and teaching in which we'd been involved. Here, too, the national Christians rallied: They provided teachers to fill in at the Bible school, ensuring that the students would be able to complete the semester's work.

"Another gratifying thing—before leaving this time, we took time to assess the work of the past five years and it became evident that evangelism, church growth, and church planting would not be substantially affected by our departure. This because of what had been happening, what God had been doing through the national church.

"The directive from our board president (C & MA), Dr. Nathan Bailey, arrived on a Sunday evening, late. So early Monday morning we met with the church leaders and told them we would be leaving. Then up until Thursday we kept in close touch with them. They evidenced a beautiful spirit right from the very beginning."

"I'll never know," says Norman Ens, "whether the Lord spoke to him in a vision or gave him a premonition or what, but one day Sin Suem, one of our church leaders, came to see me. In an uncharacteristic way, he didn't give me any greeting. He just said, 'I've changed my mind. If you missionaries want to go, it's all right with me. I won't say anything about it.'

"The very next day, the shoe dropped; word came for us to pull out. Sin Suem waited a few hours after he heard, then he came over to the house and with not a trace of bitterness or resentment or any such feeling asked, 'Will you help me find substitute teachers? We're going ahead.'

"How I admire the stature of these Christians. Here they could have been moaning and lamenting about their own very likely fate. They could have come at us with 'You're missionaries. You're serving the Lord. You came here to teach us all about Jesus and what he can do in our lives. And now, when the heat is on, when it's going to cost you something to stay with us, you run.'

"Not a word of any such thing. In fact, they were rationalizing to make us look good. 'If an ambassador directed me to do what you have to do, I would have to obey,' one of them philosophized.

"Another said to one of our missionaries, Ruth Patterson, 'God has other provinces for you to reach and tell people about Jesus.'

"The war? The enemy closing in on the city? This couldn't have been further from their minds at that moment.

"In effect, Sin Suem was saying that black day (black for us missionaries), "Now I know you have to go, and I realize this is hard on you. So let's get on with what we can do to keep things going when you are not here with us.' And he outlined what he had in mind.

" 'We can't drop the short-term Bible school; it's one-month long and we can't stop before the end of the month.' He had selected forty promising Christians for an intensive morning, afternoon, and evening course. Each Saturday they had exams. This man really knew what he was doing. He had planned this short-term school, prepared and duplicated the lesson materials, and had enlisted us missionaries to teach. It was nearing the end of the month and he wasn't about to drop it. I never saw a layman with so much enthusiasm, drive, and ability to organize and set things up the way he did. And really he didn't learn this, he didn't get it from any foreigner. He really has this gift from the Lord.

"About the exams—they're really important. Everyone's grades are recorded according to his age. Then, from somewhere, someone will scrounge around for awards for these students, a piece of clothing or whatever is available. They have a big ceremony and as the name is called, those who have made the grade come forward and receive their award with a flourish. Then they recite a verse of Scripture.

So those who have studied so hard receive due recognition, and the people who have come to honor them hear the gospel. It's just all very good.

"Only the Lord knows what it meant to us to have our fellow Christians, our Cambodian believers, handle our going as they did. Not a single one of them criticized us. It shouldn't have amazed us, for we had been fervently praying for this very thing. 'Lord,' we had been praying, 'if you want us to go, please let the national church be in agreement. Don't let them think that we are letting them down.' We had tried so hard to establish a real love relationship with them. And they came, streaming into our house until the nine o'clock curfew, and they just poured out their hearts in love. I never saw so much love expressed in four days!

"The youth committee came to our house, about four or five fellows, and they were expressing their appreciation and their love. So I asked them if I could pray with them as I did with each of the people who came to our house. I said, 'Lord, help these young fellows to really stand firm for you, and even if they have to die for you that they'll be willing to.' When I said that, all of them joined in with a hearty Amen! This is one thing they really were willing to do, and of course realizing that there was a possibility they would have to die for the Lord. This is the calibre of fellows that we have as Christians. And they are young Christians. Sometimes I'd ask them, 'How long have you been a Christian, a long time?' They would say, 'Oh, yes. A *long* time. Six months' or whatever. They think that's quite a long time already, and surely they will be able to be a shepherd to some new believer. After all, they've known the Lord for six months!

"So the Spirit of God that had been working in the

church over the preceding five years had prepared them for this hour and they accepted it like men.''

"Our experience in the sixties,'' says Gene Hall, "had taught us valuable lessons. Then, when it was necessary for us to leave the country, we sold our goods and disposed of our automobiles. And this left a bad taste in our own mouths (think what it must have done to our image as missionaries!). I personally felt like an auctioneer at that time, running around in hours of crises selling things. We determined we would never do that again. Apart from everything else, when we did return, we had nothing to start with. It wasn't much fun, for instance, making do with a sawdust-insulated box for an icebox. But I guess we had that coming to us.

"So there was none of that kind of thing in 1975!

"For the most part, we just left everything, closed the doors of our homes, and gave the keys to Cambodian brethren.

"We transferred funds to the national church and in this area, too, what a thrill it was to know there were able men to assume the responsibility. I should mention here that when we missionaries returned after the five-year interval following the forced evacuation in 1965, the national church stated in what capacity they wanted the missionaries to return: teaching, finances, literature, etc. In these three areas—Bible school, church treasurer, and publications—where large expenditures were involved, there were men of the highest calibre. We had absolutely no hesitation in handing over funds to them. Their honesty was beyond question.''

"Combined with other things,'' states Tom Wisley, "there was the factor of unusual unity among the Christian workers. I believe this has had a profound impact. I don't think that the missionaries in

Cambodia these past few years are any better or any
worse than missionaries who preceded them, or
missionaries in any other part of the world. These
Cambodian missionaries have just found themselves in
the midst of all of these changes; people are ready to
respond. And as Dr. McGavran points out, God's
Holy Spirit is the One who prepares the heart of
man. And it's our responsibility as missionaries only
to reap the harvest. So missionaries can't stand with
glowing pride and say, 'Look at what we've done.'
Because I think missionaries are making mistakes
there just as we do any place else. But somehow
these don't seem to produce the same results in
Cambodia that they have in other countries.

"Unquestionably the spirit of love and unity plays a
big part as far as the human element can be
discerned. The various organizations working there
are working in conjunction with one another. This
does not mean they're working without tension. They
are working with certain tensions between them, but
I've noticed that these have to do with important
things, not the petty things that sometimes divide us.
C & MA, the mission of record since 1923, works
with World Vision, Overseas Missionary Fellowship,
and Wycliffe. Other agencies are there, such as Bible
Literature International, who invested over $25,000 in
literature in the seventies. Now these, admittedly,
stick together and are separate from the Catholic
Relief Society (CRS) or from some of the different
organizations in Phnom Penh. But there is not the
strife there that you find in some other parts of the
missionary world. They're not spending precious time
in disputing with these other people even though they
are different. There is this uniformity that you find.
They work together. They have their staff meetings
together. They have their prayer meetings together.

They worship in the same church together. There are exceptions to this, but the general picture is of unity in the ministry, so that this has been a fine example to the national brethren.

"Within this unity factor I would include the unity of the national church with the mission. You don't see here the arguments and disagreements that frequently go along with national church and missions in much of the world today. In Cambodia there is a very beautiful working relationship between them. The missionaries are engaged primarily in leadership training. I don't know of a missionary who is involved in church planting or evangelism. They're teaching Theological Education by Extension (TEE), they are teaching in the national Bible school, they are teaching in the youth centers. They have developed other programs. For instance, the medical program is not just a matter of going out and fixing up sick people or maimed people. They have a nurses' training program they've developed to train people to run their hospitals—things like this."

The unity Tom Wisley was describing came across to me as the kind for which the Lord Jesus himself prayed: "My prayer for all of them is that they will be of one heart and mind, just as you and I are, Father—that just as you are in me and I am in you, so they will be in us, and the world will believe you sent me" (John 17:21).

That Gene Hall's goal had been accomplished—exodus with unity between the national church and the missionaries—was underscored by the following letter handed to the C & MA missionaries as they left Phnom Penh. Signed by the executive secretary of the Khmer Evangelical Church, it is evidence of the maturity of the church leaders and at the same time a plea for intercession:

Dear Missionary Friends:

" 'Where is the Lord God of Elijah?' he [Elisha] cried out. And the water parted and Elisha went across'' (2 Kings 2:14).

That verse tells how hard it was for the young man Elisha to be left behind when the old and powerful prophet of the Lord, Elijah, was taken away.

"Where is the Lord God of Elijah?" That also is the cry of the young Khmer church leaders at this moment. Elijah had been sent by God to Israel during the dark reign of its king Ahab. Despite the mighty miracles Elijah had performed, the people had not turned their hearts from sin. Then the time came for Elijah to be taken to heaven, and the young Elisha had to carry on the mission during those dark days in Israel.

But Elisha's special request for God's power was granted: " 'The spirit of Elijah rests upon Elisha!' And they went to meet him and greeted him respectfully'' (verse 15).

Dear friends, do remember us in your prayers as we Khmer Christians are left behind to continue the task in the difficult days ahead. We do need God's greater power and wisdom just as Elisha did. Please pray for us and ask God to give us the right words as we boldly tell our agonizing people about the Lord and explain to them that his salvation is for them now.

May God add many more souls to his young church in the Khmer Republic and let it grow stronger until the day of his return.

Your servant in the Lord,
Thaing Chhirc, Executive Secretary
The Khmer Evangelical Church

An important element in the exodus with unity was the fact of a home board to whom this was no new experience and who had a well-thought-out strategy for withdrawal. Nor did they leave the missionaries on their own.

The very day I left for Asia, I checked in by phone with Mr. Grady Mangham and Dr. L. L. King in Nyack, New York, only to find they had themselves departed for Asia the day before. I caught up with them in Vientiane, Laos, after they had spent considerable time in embassies in Phnom Penh and Saigon. At a briefing in the home of Laos field chairman Clement Dreger, I was privileged to hear the strategy defined (for the handwriting was on the wall for Laos also). The C & MA officials from stateside were as fully informed as is possible in such a volatile situation. This mission seemingly has the respect of ambassadors for their long service in Southeast Asia. I was tremendously impressed with their personal concern for the missionaries and their families. There were heavy hearts at that meeting, for by then five colleagues (with others from Wycliffe and a U. S. official) had been captured in Ban Me Thuot, Viet Nam, and nothing had been heard of them. So we prayed.

The four point program for evacuating made sense to me. Missionaries should go if their furlough was due within four months; if they were nearing retirement; if they had fears or felt travel would be cut off. And they should stay if it would be possible for them to launch a relief program for the nationals.

In the course of the briefing, Dr. King spelled out what was planned for air drop relief packages for the hungry, homeless refugees. Before the meeting broke up, the Laos missionaries had made individual (family) appointments for interviews the following day, concerning their reassignment to other areas.

Larry Ward of Food for the Hungry mentioned in one of his newsletters how impressed he had been with the presence of C & MA administrative personnel from the home board in the actual crisis areas.

So was I. I will never forget that meeting. One of the couples there was Dr. and Mrs. George Roffe, veteran missionaries and personal friends of the king of Laos (he and Dr. Roffe had often played chess together). What must have been in their hearts as they pondered what would be, for them, virtual exile from "home?"

It was not very long until, like their Cambodia and Viet Nam fellow missionaries, the Laos group had to activate the strategy for withdrawal and execute an exodus with unity.

It's significant that the embassies can go only so far in a time of crisis in the matter of evacuating their private citizens. This applies of course to the missionary expatriate. The ambassador can show concern (and he does); he can recommend, suggest, urge, and issue a final warning. But he cannot order the missionary to leave. Sometimes I've toyed with the idea that there may be an inherent sense that to do so would be tangling with God.

In the light of this official limitation, the mission board is wise in supporting the missionary torn by conflicting emotions (and possibly not too capable of making an objective decision) and in sending trusted advisors to confer with the missionary on this crucial issue.

The edict to leave will never be a popular directive. It helps, however, when it is accompanied by concerned, informed personal cooperation.

An article I wrote during the Bangladesh crisis gives an overview of the evacuation situation:

> This generation with its political upheaval and military coups has seen its quota of both missionary martyrs and missionary evacuees.
>
> The need to deal with this issue arises with ever greater frequency in our day: In the face of uncertain political situations, possibly confronted by certain physical danger, what does the foreign missionary do?
>
> On the home front sentiment rides high at such a time. This is commendable and understandable. At times—as in the case of the late Dr. Paul Carlson in (then) Congo or more recently, pregnant Mrs. Debbie Dortzbach, the nurse kidnaped by a liberation front group in Ethiopia—headlines scream the fact of missionary danger, to the entire nation.
>
> What about the missionaries themselves? What considerations motivate them as they try to evaluate, "Shall I accept evacuation—or shall I remain? Should I help man the front lines, or make a strategic withdrawal?"
>
> While there will always be variables, certain factors are constant.
>
> Of top priority, whatever the situation, is *sensitivity to the leading of the Lord.* God leads, generally, through his Word, through circumstances, and through giving a sense of inner peace as the individual steps out in the direction in which he believes the Lord is leading. There is a corresponding uneasiness of spirit which must be construed as a "Stop!" The Lord may be saying, "Go," to some while he says, "Stay," to others. If each is following his

leading, then let not other Christians who are far
from the actual situation sit in judgment on the
missionary, whatever his action in the face of
confusion and danger.

Another consideration is, What effect will the
missionary's decision have on the national
believers, some of whom may be new converts?
There have been numerous occasions when the
best thing a missionary could do in the interests
of the people he came to minister to, is to leave
their area. Not to do so may be hazardous for
the national Christians. At other times the
courage displayed by the missionary remaining
has put spiritual iron into the soul of the
national.

Also to be considered is the type of missionary
service. For a medical missionary—doctor or
nurse—to flee from personal danger at the very
time his skills are most needed, as, for instance,
in times when many are injured through violence
and war, would violate his professional code,
apart from the spiritual aspect. Then, too,
sometimes what appears to threaten as a
long-term situation may turn out to be of brush
fire duration and the missionary is glad that he
remained on the job.

Were we to ask some missionaries what
motivated them to remain when the choice
became necessary, they might share with us their
belief that *God works in spectacular ways in times of
crisis.* Viet Nam was surely such a scene. If, as
C. S. Lewis declared, "Pain is God's megaphone
for a deaf world," then turmoil and war in
foreign lands are many times God's means of
solidifying the work of the missionaries, as well
as strengthening the national Christian.

When God is clearly leading and the missionary stays at his post or retreats to a safe area from which to carry on, the national believer sees faith in action as the missionary demonstrates his willingness to hazard his life, if need be, for God.

The other side of this coin is when the missionary is acting on his own initiative rather than seeking God's leading. This is not always a matter of supreme dedication. Sometimes it is natural stick-to-it-iveness carried to excess. There needs to be flexibility that allows one not only to pray, *"Show me thy way,"* but causes the individual to *walk in the way God is revealing,* even though this be contrary to his own will in the situation.

More than one missionary will testify that it was after he had been led to leave one area due to hostile conditions, that the Lord led him to a place of much greater service and satisfaction.

Missionaries, like all Christians, are in God's hands. To a greater degree than we who are not foreign missionaries, they may be called to witness "by life or by death." Nevertheless, the safest place in all the universe for a Christian is the center of God's will.[1]

[1] Jeanette Lockerbie, "The Missionary—Martyr or Evacuee?" *Psychology for Living,* July/August 1971, p. 5.

Missionaries
in Limbo

When is a missionary not a missionary?

When he is an evacuee.

The above might pass as a riddle if that was what
we were dealing with. The life experience is infinitely
more tantalizing, however, than the most obscure
riddle. Regardless of what life on the mission field
might bring of trial, frustration, or danger, I have yet
to meet one missionary who if the choice were solely
his/hers would choose to be evacuated. Nevertheless,
there are times when discretion is the better part of
valor.

Mission boards and agencies have varying policies
and mandates concerning their foreign personnel.
Circumstances also dictate differing approaches to the
dilemma. In any case, the possibility of evacuation
because of a crisis can't help but produce intense
trauma for those concerned. Frequently the hardest

thing to bear is the day-to-day uncertainty. God does not usually flash Stop or Go signs.

I was greatly moved, therefore, by the story told to me by Chuck and Sally Keller of Wycliffe's Summer Institute of Linguistics program. Challenged by the need for workers in Cambodia, they went there in October 1973 to a place called Pailin. The hub of the economy there was precious stones. Sally and Chuck went digging for other gems—a tribal language whereby they could give the Brao people the gospel in their own tongue.

Located as they were some 275 miles from the capital, things appeared quite tranquil. Nevertheless news on the BBC, Voice of America, and the Far East Broadcasting Company stations sounded grim, all the more so for Americans, with the likelihood of the cutoff of U. S. aid to Cambodia. And Phnom Penh was a two-day trip; the roads could be cut off any time. What should they do? One day they felt they should stay, the next it seemed wise to leave.

"At this time," Sally relates, "our kids' favorite Bible story was the flight to Egypt. Oh, it had nothing to do with the current situation," she hastened to inform me. "John and Jody had, for weeks, night after night wanted this same Bible story. 'Tell us 'bout Joseph 'n Mary and the baby Jesus 'n the *angel*,' our little blond, John, would ask eagerly, and Jody's dark eyes would glisten in anticipation. Then one night as I was retelling it for what seemed to me the hundredth time, it came to me, *This is sort of like our own situation.* And I pondered, How we would really appreciate the appearance of an angel with a specific message for us to leave!"

In a way, God did send his "angel" in the form of a new sense of urgency on Chuck's part that they should leave (and he had not, till then, been one bit impressed that it was time for them to leave). Sally shared with me that they read with new meaning 2 Corinthians 2:8, 9: "I think you ought to know, dear brothers, about the hard time we went through in Asia. We were really crushed and overwhelmed, and feared we would never live through it . . . but that was good, for then we put everything into the hands of God, who alone could save us. . . ."

Frequently it is the home board (rather than any angel), operating from the platform of knowledge gained from embassy officials, who decree the when and how of evacuating their missionaries. While appreciating the board's concern for their safety and bowing to their decree, many a missionary has his own personal battle over the issue. I heard of one man who upon evacuation from Cambodia to Bangkok walked the streets of that city all night, wrestling with his emotions.

The question in the heart and indeed on the lips of some of these Cambodian missionaries was: Why, God? Why remove us just when your Spirit is working there as never before?

"At first," says field chairman Gene Hall, "the directive from Nyack (C & MA headquarters) to leave just tore up our missionaries. It took time for some to get the victory over this. Yet after the initial shock, we sensed a beautiful spirit. We realized that God is sovereign in our lives, that we are not the victim of circumstances."

Said Mr. and Mrs. Ens, "We just constantly kept telling the Lord we were depending on him to move us; we felt he had called us to Cambodia and he would have to call us out. Nevertheless, when the directive came from our mission president, we took that as the Lord's direction for us, but it was hard, extremely hard to leave. We had four days to get out, and we just had to believe that somehow this was the Lord's will for us."

Dr. Dean Kroh shared his feelings: "Since we've been out, we find a heaviness in our hearts—as if a loved one had died. Worse, really, for we know that the loved one in the Lord goes to be with him at death and this is a real comfort. But we know that so many in Cambodia do not know the Lord, and those who do will certainly suffer a great deal when the Khmer Rouge take over.

"We try to laugh over something, but right in the middle of it this sadness deep inside—well, you just don't get over it. Maybe this will lift in time. But right now this is the way we feel."

Dr. Kroh's wife, Esther, added, "Another thing that is a burden to us is our having such good meals and knowing there are thousands in Phnom Penh that have only a handful of rice. It's really hard sometimes to enjoy our meals. We're meeting every morning for prayer and this is the main burden of our prayer for both the Christians and the non-Christians. We're thinking especially of the brand new Christians, that these daily needs will not discourage them; we're praying the Lord will meet their needs."

It was hot in Bangkok ("We call this the 'cruel' month," one of the students in my writing seminar informed me). But the oppressive heat was not the cruelest thing plaguing the evacuated missionaries. They were heartsick. When not on guard, they could be seen just staring into space.

A missionary attending my seminar brought to class one day this poem, in which she expresses what she sensed in her fellow-missionaries, the evacuees:

We fled, Lord
From our anguished people

and their devastated land,
Our pillow's wet with tears.
O, God, why did this happen—
Aren't you in control?
They're your people, Lord
And ours—
These captive Khmers
Who had such faith.
A mighty harvest came—
Now this!
How could you, God?
How can they praise you for this war,
These stumbling weary refugees,
Hungry, desolate, hopeless, dying.
They'll curse you, God,
They'll rave and shake their fists at heaven!
God, we've been here these few days,
But Bangkok's not our home
They do not need us here.
This place is one big sauna—
We sweat and read black headlines
While Cambodia sinks in despair.
O help us, God.
We flounder in our tears.
We act like walkers in their sleep.
O Lord, have mercy.
Give our people there
The strength to reap that golden harvest
Ripe—that we have left behind.

Ruth Perkins, C & MA
Udorn, Thailand

Scarcely had the Cambodian missionary contingent begun to accept their being evacuees when with stunning suddenness, Saigon fell and the Vietnamese missionaries were arriving to swell the number already in Bangkok.

The C & MA Guest House had a population explosion. And what was the big event in their day? Not the bell summoning them to breakfast, lunch, or dinner, excellent though the fare was. Not the shopping in fabulous Bangkok. Not the cooling break in a nearby swimming pool to which they had access. No, it was none of these.

Actually two things made these uprooted missionaries spring to life: One, the news on someone's shortwave radio. Everything stopped and those who did not have a set crowded close to hear the nearest radio. This was their link with their real life; it could just possibly be word about their captured colleagues at Ban Me Thuot, or some new move in Phnom Penh or Saigon. Everything else could wait.

The second vitalizer was the sound of wheels and brakes on the gravel driveway. Talk would cease as someone dashed to the window to call over his shoulder, "It's—" The word passed quickly as those on the scene rushed out to greet the new arrival. Then, as eager to share as the others were to hear, the missionary who had been privileged to make a return trip to his field gave himself wholly to the absorbed listeners. I can see them yet as Gene Hall arrived, having spent Easter Sunday with the Khmer brethren in Phnom Penh; and Reg Reimer with his gruesome report from Saigon.

How did the displaced missionaries spend their time? It would seem this would be a problem to men and women who on the job never had enough hours in any day. Some were in a holding pattern awaiting reassignment; others had children in boarding school and would remain in Asia till the end of the school year, then head back to their home country.

Those engaged in translation had brought their

work with them. I frequently observed the Kellers pouring over their notes, one or the other busy at the typewriter with the Cambodian characters. Sally had been working on a medical dictionary for use in training national nurses.

Literally hours were spent on the telephone as, deeply concerned for the safety of certain Christians, some missionaries contacted embassy officials. I was impressed that these men and women just didn't give up. As long as there was one more even slim possibility, they doggedly pursued it. And there was great rejoicing when a young mother and her three small children arrived safely; her husband, a Cambodian serviceman, had been sent to the United States for training. A tribal young woman, she had ten years earlier managed to escape from a dangerous situation and had walked through the forest to safety. Now much telephoning between Bangkok and Washington eventuated in her being permitted to join her husband in America. It was as if she had been everybody's family; her children were everybody's children. Such was the spirit of love and warmth and concern (even while each family had its own problems). It was beautiful. It must surely have made the angels smile.

And how deep was the sadness when word came that someone really endangered was not permitted to leave Cambodia (some, it must be said, voluntarily refused possible evacuation, choosing rather to remain and continue their Christian witness).

Some missionaries were nurturing Cambodian evacuees living temporarily in Bangkok. A heartwarming scene occurred when Mr. and Mrs. Norman Ens appeared at the C & MA Guest House, each carrying a lovely Cambodian child. These were two of a group of babies airlifted by World Vision and later flown to the U. S. by the American military. In the interim they were cared for in a Christian home, by Christian volunteers. One day, the Enses must have decided that the babies needed some loving in Cambodian. So they went and talked to the little ones in their own language, then brought the two to show off to us. It did something to me—the insight of this couple who recognized this very special need and did something about it.

There was some quipping about the verse "taking joyfully the spoiling of our goods," but not once did I hear any lamenting or complaining. One practical person posed the question, "I'm willing to take the loss joyfully enough, but what do I live on for the next three years?" (She had just lately arrived on her field with her four years' supplies.)

Ted and Marjorie Cline (United Bible Societies) wrote in their prayer letter, "The prospect of setting up housekeeping in North America from 'scratch' is a rather daunting one for expatriates such as we . . . We expect to give the secondhand stores and the Goodwill shops in the area a new lease on life!"

Significantly, what some did moan and groan about was that they had left good equipment, typewriters, business machines, etc. "My lovely new typewriter!" one of the secretaries bemoaned. "And to think the Communists will get it."

Perhaps the greatest engrossment was just listening to one another, and what healing that must have brought. For where else would they find truly empathetic listeners who would let them talk the grief out of their system and not get impatient? (One of the most poignant comments I've heard in a long time was that made by a missionary on furlough, "Nobody wants to *hear*. Oh, they say, 'How are things over there?' but before I can answer, they're on another

subject. Or someone says, 'You must have so much
to tell; I'd love to hear sometime'—and that's the end
of it.'' And this particular missionary really does have
something to tell and a most interesting, lively way of
telling it when he has the chance.)

Then, for those with a writing flair, there was my
two-week seminar/workshop which gave scope for
writing the experiences so fresh in their minds. And
selling their manuscripts, moreover!

At the Evangelical Church in Bangkok, emotions
really showed that first Sunday morning in April. A
guest speaker, Dr. Robert Frost, gave a fine message.
''God acts—the enemy reacts—and God
counteracts.'' I suspect these three points linger in
my mind because of the association with the
circumstances under which I heard them.

The pastor, Rev. David Anderson, with rare
sensitivity allowed for the feelings which he realized
gripped his congregation. He called for prayer first
for the missing missionaries, C & MA and Wycliffe, a
prayer fittingly led by Rev. Grady Mangham, Jr.,
C & MA secretary for Asia, whose presence spoke of
the Board's personal concern for their missionaries in
traumatic times. Again, focus was placed on the fact
that God knows and cares, as prayer was offered for
the Cambodian believers and for the missionaries
whose hearts were bleeding because they had to leave
their work and their loved fellow Christians. And a
third call to prayer—this time for the Vietnamese
missionaries and those they had left behind. And not
forgotten were the children of all these uprooted
missionaries, many of them away in boarding schools,
thinking their own thoughts and fighting their private
battles over possible changes in their life situation.

Tears flowed that morning and no one was ashamed
of them. Except perhaps for one or two whose

background had programmed them to think that tears
were unspiritual, a sign of non-submission to the will
of God, and these apologized afterwards for "not
being able to keep from crying"; but in general we
gave vent to our deeply aroused feelings. These were
our brethren, our family—Cambodian, Vietnamese,
American, Canadian, British, and European. Some of
us there that morning had not been present to rejoice
with them in their rejoicings; but this day we could
weep with them in their hour of sorrow.

A rather strange group occupied some front pews
in that service, a number of nuns in their habit,
unusual enough to cause the preacher (and Grady
Mangham) to blink a time or two. This was a
contingent of Catholic sisters who had been in
Cambodia, far from the city, for years without ever
returning to their homes. They had never even seen a
plane before being evacuated, and we learned that
they decidedly did not want to leave the country.

In every respect it was a church service to
remember. One announcement, for example, was a
plea for baby cribs, cots, blankets, and equipment for
a group of orphans being flown into Bangkok and
who would be cared for there pending an airlift to the
United States. The call was also for nurses and other
people who could help care for these babies. I hadn't
heard an announcement quite like that before!

And then it was time for the Lord's Supper.

"We may run out of Communion cups," the pastor
cautioned his elders.

Maybe so, I thought, *but we will not run out of
Communion.* The very air was charged with the
presence of the Holy Spirit.

Not quite understanding the reddened eyes and the
open tears, some little worshipers stared in a kind of
awe. I think many of them will remember that

service. I know I always will.

Later along the way I met some of these
missionaries. In Hong Kong Mr. and Mrs. Paul
Ellison shared with me some of their feelings on this
see-saw service for the Lord. For them, evacuation,
while frustrating, nevertheless gave time for needed
translation in which they were engaged. So three
months in Bangkok would bring its own satisfaction.
That is, until the assignment came to work in Guam
with the newly arrived refugees. It's said of Paul
Ellison, who was ten months old when his missionary
parents took him to Cambodia, that his Cambodian is
so perfect that on the telephone (when he isn't
personally identified) he is easily mistaken for a native
Cambodian.

"It's not where we are," said Paul Ellison, "it's
what we are doing—more, it's what we are doing in
the light of what God wants us to do at a particular
time that counts." Admirable dedication. But there
are more than spiritual ramifications in all the moves.
How to keep mentally ready—how to know what to
have on hand when you don't know God's next move
for you (or your mission board's). And what about
the practicalities of clothes and other necessities? No
use arriving someplace to immediately be less than
effective because of certain "not haves". Yet money
and time to shop, and space allotted (one suitcase, for
instance) are all factors.

(I heard fascinating snatches of conversation about
"what we grabbed up when we had to evacuate" and
I listened as one after another rationalized why they
had brought out the things they did, why they were
important by contrast with seemingly more
immediately practical items. This made me go back in
my thoughts to when my daughter Jeannie and her
colleague, Lynn Silvernale, had to make a hasty exit

from Chittagong, Bangladesh, during the war there, *with one American Tourister totebag between them.* When this came out in a newsletter, much interest was engendered. Just about everybody wanted to know what two girls, fleeing from bombs (and worse) would elect to carry within the limitation of half a tote bag each. Because of this inordinate interest, I asked my daughter to answer their questions in her book, *On Duty in Bangladesh*—which she did.)

I heard of a family where the wife had been evacuated first. The husband's directive to leave came with just a half-hour's notice. "The clothes were in the washing machine," he said, "and all I could do was turn off the machine and leave them and beat it to the airport." Not much chance there to decide which suitcase and what to put in it.

Missionaries in limbo. For them it takes probably more dedication, more spiritual stamina, more waiting on the Lord, than when they're on the front line confronting the enemy of men's souls. It's their own inner being they're all too often doing battle with.

The family cannot escape the effects of the uprooting. Pleasant and exciting as it is to return to their homeland, this is not "home" to them. And anyway, what will they do? Particularly the missionaries evacuated from Cambodia and Viet Nam would be indulging in fantasy if they sat and waited for the mission door to open there in the forseeable future. So what next? And where?

Months may elapse in which a family lives in suitcases, never quite sure what is the best step to take. While they wait on God, these Christians need a special brand of understanding. The children, out of their element, may act just like that; they may not live up to the expectations of church hosts and hostesses.

This is a good time for the rest of us to practice the Golden Rule, to put ourselves in the missionaries' place (if we can stretch our imagination that far), to go the second mile in making them feel comfortable and accepted and wanted. Not that these missionaries look to be treated as something special. Far from it. They just need the comfort of knowing that the people in the churches care that their hearts are bleeding and that the only thing they really want is to be back with the people to whom God called them. It will help if we tell them we sense this. Say the words, "We're so glad to have you, even though we know you would rather be back in (whatever the country)." The missionary will bless you for your understanding and there will be healing for his hurt.

Missionaries in limbo? They are still missionaries.

12

The Laymen— God's VIPs

Turn in here—it's God's Place
Refugees. A lump of humanity.

For many of us in this decade, the word has become too familiar, has lost its poignance. We may even (God forgive us) view the "refugee situation" as another possible bid for funds "when we're already giving to so many causes." The word "refugee" conjures up images of long strings of disorganized, poverty-stricken, homeless, and seemingly aimless, anonymous people. Pregnant women. Tired soldiers. Disillusioned teen-agers. Bewildered old people. A hodge-podge of household possessions, all that can be carried or loaded on a push- or oxcart. Frequently the father is off on the fighting lines, so women and children make up most of the pitiable pilgrimage.

Whither are they bound? Mostly they have no destination. Unless in their minds there is a vague unmapped location named "safety."

For some fortunate ones there is such a place. It's "God's Place."

The host of God's Place, Sin Soum, is just one of the notable Christian laymen who were front-line in God's strategy for the Khmer Republic.

A schoolteacher, Sin Soum had himself been a refugee.

Always an ambitious person, he kept on learning and became a teacher of agriculture in the northwest city of Battambang. It was there the bottom fell out of his world when with his wife and six children, he had to flee from the Vietcong as they moved in with their reign of terror. Teachers were always early targets for the VC. So to save their lives, he and his family joined the thousands of desperate refugees.

Life in Phnom Penh, where they sought to remake their lives, was a constant struggle for survival. Jobs were not plentiful; food was scarce. Sin Soum began to feel hopeless and depressed.

As a thirteen-year-old, like so many other young men, he had studied for a time in a Buddhist temple. But Buddhism had no answers for him now. The Buddhist monks were themselves begging, even from the refugees. To Sin Soum, his life that had seemed so promising appeared now to be a dead-end street.

It was while he was in this frame of mind that he saw announcements, "Hear the Good News for Cambodia," advertising a Stan Mooneyham crusade. Sin Soum determined to find out more. If he ever needed good news, it was then. But when he went to the auditorium, there was such a crowd that he didn't get in. He stalked off in an angry mood.

But the next evening he was there early. He couldn't know then how far-reaching was his decision to return. But God knew.

"Everything I heard was new to me," he relates.
That evening Mooneyham, speaking through an
interpreter to a crowded audience, told the simple
gospel story—the birth, life, death, and resurrection
of Jesus Christ. That Jesus is *alive*—this is what took
hold of so many Cambodians who heard it for the
first time. And that night, among the many who
reached out to receive Christ was Sin Soum. In fact,
he was the first on his feet at the invitation. He
hurried home to tell his wife, "I have found the
living Savior, I have peace." Kao, his wife, was not
immediately impressed, but a few months later she
too received Jesus as her Savior.

Not only was Sin Soum's soul saved; his marriage,
which was rocky, was also beautifully rebuilt.

It's a phenomenon of the movement of the Spirit in
Khmer land that the new converts felt almost
immediately a responsibility to reach their own
people. No waiting until they had attended personel
evangelism classes or had mastered a few books of the
Bible. From the hopelessness and deadness of
Buddhism, in the crucible of war and death, they had
found Jesus Christ. And they were not going to keep
quiet about it! (I can't help contrasting these
enthusiasts for the Resurrection with what we read
about the disciples: First they disputed that it was just
"idle tales" told by a probably hysterical woman; see
Luke 24:11. But let me be fair. They did get into the
spirit when the first shock wore off, and if every
generation of believers had done what they
accomplished in their time, the world would have
been evangelized long ago.)

For the Cambodian who met Jesus and believed in
him, every day was Easter.

It was to share his faith with the refugees, to let
them get in on the good news, that Sin Soum moved

his family out from the city to an area called New Phnom Penh, a section set aside for the mounting hordes of refugees. It was practically a desert, a wilderness. Sin Soum built a shelter, one big room, for his family. His wife had to go a long way to bring water every day, and there was no market.

They were a beautiful team for God, Sin Soum and his wife. Together they daily witnessed to their neighbors. On Sunday they regularly cleared things out of their house. Then asking God to bless them, they invited people until forty or fifty crowded in each Sunday. Soon they were aiming for a church.

Not only so, but Sin Soum began posting a Christian (often Kao herself) to stand at the crossroads where the refugees streamed by. The weary people were gently urged to "turn in here—it's God's Place; he will be with you. He will take care of you."

Hundreds came. They found warmth and love. Many said, "We've fled from so many places already; we have never felt this satisfaction in our hearts before, a feeling that somebody cares for us."

Is it any wonder that so many of those people accepted Christ right in that refugee camp? There was a wonderful sense of optimism, reported Marie Ens. It didn't have the air that you'd expect in such a camp. It was as if in spite of their situation, there was hope. The children were singing and playing, and when the children are happy, then the parents are happy too. They were singing praises to the Lord. They were optimistic in their outlook even though they did not always have enough to eat. Many times they would have to stretch their rice by making it into a porridge. But they said they didn't care whether they ate so well or not, they wanted to stay at this place because their hearts were ministered to. This was something they wouldn't get at most camps.

Even the grounds surrounding the church area have a cared-for look at this layman's church. For Sin Soum brought all of his knowledge of growing plants and trees, all his agricultural know-how with him into his service for the Lord. You rarely saw him ride back home without a bush or a tree or a plant strapped to his motorcycle. He felt that God's Place should look beautiful.

This church (they call it Horeb) is so indigenous that they wouldn't dream of running around at Christmas to see who's going to give them money to buy candy for the children. They've thought ahead and grown rice around their church property. From the rice there's a special sweet they make, and they serve this as a Christmas treat. They spend little money, but they manage to have enough for everybody.

Sin Soum just keeps adding little houses or shacks for the refugees. And every night of the week they have services for them, for the children first with lots of singing.

"Praise the Lord," wrote Dr. Kroh to C & MA in New York. "It's thrilling to see Sin Soum work. I went out to New Phnom Penh to hold a clinic for the first time in the home of a couple who put their trust in the Lord just two weeks ago. Sin Soum says a revival has hit the area."

He's not very old, this fantastic Christian layman—just thirty-five, but the people respect him, they love him, and they're willing to follow him. Towards nightfall he lights the lantern and invites the people to a service. There he talks to them about Christ—these people to whom death is so ever-present, for almost all of them have lost a family member through the months of enemy action. The very air is permeated with love and a sense of security; the peoples' fears are calmed through the Word of God spoken to them as they get ready to go to sleep.

One night an old woman came to Sin Soum pleading, "Teacher, don't leave us; we want you to be here with us."

"Don't worry, Granny," he reassured her, "I have a friend and he has many men. They will stand all around us and guard us."

"Where are they?" the fearful old woman wanted to know, "and who is he, this friend of yours?"

"My friend is Jesus, and he has many, many angels."

The woman went on her way, her fears set at rest.

The missionaries shared the same dangers as the refugees and they, too, needed the comfort and assurance that they have Jesus for their friend and that he has many angels. I recall Mrs. Dean Kroh's telling me what the Word of God meant to her and her doctor husband at such times:

"It's two o'clock in the morning and the bombs are dropping about every three minutes; they'll keep it up for hours and you can just sense them coming closer and closer. It seems the Lord speaks just the right promises to your heart. At different times over these last two and a half years Psalm 27 and Psalm 91, for instance, have helped us. We all know what they are and what a comfort they've been to God's people through the centuries. But in times like these, the verses come to life. You picture David in the situation when he wrote these Psalms and you find yourself adapting them to your own situation, or your suffering friends. The verses that have specially come alive for me are these:

The Lord is my light, and my salvation:
whom shall I fear? the Lord is the strength
of my life; of whom shall I be afraid?
Though a host should encamp against me, my
heart shall not fear: though war should arise
against me, in this will I be confident.

The angel of the Lord encampeth round about
them that fear him, and delivereth them.

He that dwelleth in the secret place of the
Most High shall abide under the shadow of the
Almighty.
Thou shalt not be afraid for the terror by night.
For he shall give his angels charge over thee,
to keep thee in all thy ways.
(Psalm 27:1, 3; 34:7; 91:1, 5, 11 KJV)

One night Sin Soum was telling the people that if
they became afraid in the night when the rockets
started going over, they should call on the name of
the Lord to help them and then Jesus would protect
them. And he added, "That's all you have to do. You
don't have to pay any money [in their former religion
they had to pay, pay, pay]. You don't have to pay
anything at all," he repeated. "All you need to do is
pray to God.

"If that's too hard for you, if it's too much to ask
of you just to call on the Lord—then just go ahead
and die!" And they all laughed because they
understood he said this as a joke, to lift them up and
amuse them. Then he asked, "Now how many of you
will do that tonight when you begin to feel afraid;
how many of you will call on Jesus to protect you and
help you?" And of course they all raised their hands,
indicating that they would.

Sin Soum ministered to his people in other ways

too; sometimes just by his kindly interest or a passing word.

"How are you, Grandfather?"

"Have you had enough to eat today, Granny?"

"Oh, yes, you're doing a good job building that wall."

"Your children are well now?"

Just taking time to walk around and chat with them did so much to bring comfort and encouragement to the refugees at God's Place.

The missionaries tell the story of a woman, a widow living alone, who started to dig for water. Usually the digging had to be at least ten meters in order to strike water. But this woman (her husband had been killed in the war) prayed, "Lord, you know that I am an old woman and I can't dig very much."

At *two* meters she struck a well of water. "It's a miracle from God in answer to prayer," she exclaimed. She was so thankful that the Lord had heard and answered her prayer, that she would not draw any water for her own needs until first her well had been used as a place of baptism. So fifteen to twenty people were baptized at the widow's well that God had given her.

It was here Sin Soum built a church. Because he had stepped out on faith and opened up this new area, when the Khmer Rouge began burning villages to the north of his church, there was a place for the fearful villagers to flee to—God's Place.

It has become a hive of life and love and vitality and security for the refugees. And there's a market there—the *Jesus* Market. Everybody—taxi drivers, anybody—can tell you how to get to the Jesus Market.

When Gene Hall returned to Phnom Penh for a few days before the final pullout of all missionaries,

Sin Soum told him there were four to five thousand
in the camp, with around 1,000 of them Christians.

Gene says there's warmth, love, teaching of the
children; rice is provided, and a medical clinic. And
without fail, the daily services. "You should hear
those people pray!" Gene enthuses. (Prayer had not
seemingly been a major emphasis among the believers
until then.) "I tell you these people really know God;
those refugees really know the Bible. And they can't
be beat for witnessing. No question about their
sincerity and their knowledge of the Lord!"

This is Sin Soum. This is God's Place.

The man who said hello
War-marked refugees in Phnom Penh are often
startled to find gifts of fish, rice, salt, mosquito nets,
and clothes presented to them by countrymen who
are Christians.

Were the refugees to ask who was directing this
relief work, they would be even more mystified. He
is a well-dressed, quietly assured young man who
used to have a high-ranking job with Shell Oil. His
name is Minh Thien Voan (just Voan to his friends),
and his name, fittingly enough, means "heavenly
messenger."

Voan's first big step toward his present usefulness
resulted from his uncommon diligence as a student,
which earned him a scholarship to the University of
Georgia in 1962. There he became friends with a
Campus Crusade worker, George Jefferson, and was
impressed with this Christian. But Voan's response to
Jefferson's testimony was colored by his Buddhist
background. And his conversion was certainly not
run-of-the-mill.

Many of us as Christians have a tendency to

squeeze the process of conversion into our own mold. We have a working formula and we don't want anyone to interfere with the mix: "Bow your head," "raise your hand," "come forward and be counseled." Nothing amiss with any of these, unless we become totally locked into this pattern as a path to Jesus. All too often we take a dim view of the genuineness of the conversion of a person whose experience, in our opinion, is a little offbeat. We forget that the Holy Spirit marches to no one's drum. He has the divine right to be different.

Jesus is God and he is to be worshiped in spirit and in truth. But there is nothing static, nothing stereotyped about the way in which he comes to the individual who seeks him. And he does not have to give account of his methods. It's refreshing to be reminded, in the life of a convert, that the triune God is original. Minh Voan of Cambodia is a prime example. Invited by Jefferson to a Bible study, with the politeness characteristic of his people, he didn't voice what was in his mind: *If you think you're going to get me to believe in your Jesus, you are mistaken.* He did attend the meeting, however—somewhat hesitantly, to be sure—and the study centered around John 3:16: "For God so loved the world, that he gave his only begotten Son, that whosoever believeth in him should not perish, but have everlasting life" (KJV).

The reluctant foreign student could not get these words out of his mind. He wrestled with them long on his bed, far into the night. Finally he prayed, "O God, you know how hard it would be for me to accept you, coming from Buddhism. But if you can help me with this problem, I want to accept you as my Savior."

Voan relates that following that prayer, "I had a strange sense that someone was in the room with me.

I looked all around and there was no one that I could
see. Still I was certain someone was there with me. I
didn't know what to do. So I just said, 'Hello!' That
was the beginning of my wonderful relationship with
Jesus Christ.''

In 1968, Voan received his Master's degree in
engineering and returned to the Khmer Republic. He
sought out what was then the only Protestant church
in the city of Phnom Penh, the Evangelical Church
that dated back to the early missionaries in the 1920s.
His arrival opened up a whole new dimension of
witness for the struggling, small, beleaguered
congregation. To that time the church had
concentrated almost all its evangelistic efforts on the
farming class and the uneducated people of the city.
Voan was able to attract the university students and
the influential leaders in government.

When he went home to visit his parents, however,
he found them strongly opposed to their son's
changing to a new religion, turning from Buddhism.
He was their oldest son. "Who," they asked, "would
offer sacrifices for us when we die?"

It was an unhappy situation for a loving son. But
despite the continued opposition, he lived a gracious
Christian life before his parents and prayed earnestly
for them. And God honored his witness. The day
came when his mother reached out in her own way to
Jesus.

"I don't know who you are, God," she prayed,
"but my son knows you. I like what I see in him, and
I want to know you as my son does." But not yet did
she accept Jesus as her Savior.

A strategy that upgraded the church's image was
the starting of a language school by Voan and the
church leaders. Government officials, university
students, and businessmen all wanted to attend and

learn English. And there, as he taught English, Voan witnessed about Jesus Christ. Scores of students and other city residents were won to the Lord.

Voan's arrival in Phnom Penh coincided with an awakened concern by the Christians to have more than one church in the city. Members voted and began to move out to start new churches, until there were eleven congregations.

A shortage of pastors caused the church leaders to turn to their laymen for help. Voan, along with two other laymen, accepted responsibility for one of these new churches, and after a while it had the largest attendance of all.

In mid-1973, Voan gave up his position with Shell Oil to become World Vision's deputy director for the Khmer Republic. "The only thing that satisfies my heart is serving Jesus Christ," he says.

Voan is also an active Gideon. On a trip with the World Vision team and missionary Merle Graven to a large (40,000) refugee camp, Voan presented the general in charge with a lovely New Testament in Cambodian.

Because of his open Christian witness, he is an endangered person and he certainly qualified for evacuation as conditions deteriorated. He refused to leave, however, simply stating, "My people need me, for so many of them, including some of my own family, do not yet know Jesus."

I heard about this man and his selfless determination to remain with his people at any cost. I admired him as an outstanding Christian.

Some weeks later I was privileged to spend time in the refugee camp at Camp Pendleton Marine Base in California. There the full impact of Voan's devotion to Christ hit me. For there I met and talked with a beautiful young Cambodian woman. As we visited

together, a smiling baby girl on the mother's lap
played with my pencil; two other little ones, a boy
and a girl, skipped and played around us stopping
periodically for a sip from the Coke bottle. They
were Voan's wife, Theri, and their children. This
woman refugee's husband was half a world away
enduring—who knows what? Theri, with her children,
was housed at the headquarters of World Vision. My
meeting her was another "chance encounter"; she
was spending a day with her father, a refugee waiting
to be cleared before going to his new home in the
United States.

Did she complain that she was there, her husband
so far away? Did she fret about having the sole care
of three small children? Did she sigh over her
uncertain future? No. Her thinking as she expressed
it to me matched her husband's: *How could he leave
Cambodia when so many—some his own family—did not
yet know Jesus?*

Besides being beautiful, this young woman is a
talented linguist, speaking, besides her native
Cambodian, French, English, Chinese, and
Vietnamese.

We talked about the great turning to Christ in her
land and she reiterated what others had told me:
"Many Cambodians believed. They had heard the
words of Jesus, but this was the foreigner's religion
and it made the king very angry that people were
forsaking Buddhism, so he was putting them in
prison. Now it is possible for them to believe in Jesus
and to tell others about him."

I left Mrs. Voan with a prayer in my heart that God
in his infinite wisdom would reunite the man who had
said "hello" to Jesus with his wife and little children.
At the same time, I greatly admired her spirit and her
attitude.

Her father, too, with his daughter as interpreter, told me how he came to know Christ. As I was walking away with my Marine escort, the father asked his daughter to tell us that in Camp Pendleton, his people were finding that Americans are loving and kind. "And," he added, "this is a moment when Cambodia needs love and warmth."

If in far-off Cambodia Minh Voan could know it, his heart would surely be comforted to realize that his lovely young wife, his three little children, and his father-in-law are in such good hands. But when I asked his wife, Theri, "Have you heard from your husband?" a faraway look stole into her dark eyes. "No. Not for a *long* time," she answered softly. "I've had just one letter from him."

What of Voan himself?

Only God knows. Minh Voan had prayed, "God, you know it will be hard." He couldn't know then how hard. He had counted the cost in refusing evacuation for the sake of winning souls to Christ. And what had that one letter told? Minh Voan had led his father, his mother, and his three sisters to Christ!

Cambodia's Christian soldier
Influential Khmer Christian laymen were found in many professions. Notable among them is Army Major Chhirc. He somehow seems to be there just when he is needed. For example, Rev. Isaac Scott, Overseas Missionary Fellowship director, shares this experience, so rare in "normal" Christian circles but apparently almost a one-a-day occurrence among the zealous Cambodians:

Scott was at the Phnom Penh airport being checked through immigration when one of the airline

stewardesses in the reception area approached him.
She wanted to know about Christianity and expressed
her own interest and her desire to know how she
could find out more. She asked where she might go in
Phnom Penh to find out.

This stewardess was a Cambodian herself, so she
would normally spend time there in Phnom Penh.

"I was just ready to board my flight," says Scott,
"so I could have only a short chat with her. But
Major Chhirc happened to be there at the airport and
he came up to speak to me. I was able to introduce
the stewardess to him, and he answered her questions
and made arrangements for them to meet at Bethany
Church."

Major Chhirc is, as mentioned earlier in the book,
a third generation Christian; he is not one of the
products of the New Life upsurge. Rather, he has
been and is a leader among the Christians.

In February 1971, a missionary chairman wrote, "A
new level of leadership has now taken over with an
aggressive program of evangelism . . . You might be
interested to know that one of these is Chhirc who
has manifested a spirit of dedication seldom seen in
the life of any Christian. He is now a major in the
Cambodian army and on the staff working with
General Lon Nol."

Granted a scholarship for a Ph. D. program in
England, Chhirc returned home before completing his
work because of a great spiritual burden for his
people.

Though brought up in a Christian home, apparently
Chhirc did not make a commitment to Jesus Christ
until he was grown up and serving his country in the
army.

In a letter to Mr. and Mrs. Clifford Westergren,
dated July 2, 1962, Chhirc wrote:

. . . In this letter I want to give a testimony to my dear Lord Jesus about the Spirit of God working in my life, as follows:

Do you remember a note you sent to me on November 4, telling me about a word of Jesus, Luke 9:60–62? That verse corresponded exactly to my thinking . . .

Now I would like to tell you that he (Jesus) has found me, not that I find him but only my Lord Jesus has found me because he doesn't want me to die. Praise the Lord!

Before, I wanted to keep "my" honor, "my" glory, and "my" life for myself; but now he told me to give all that's mine to him and him only, so that he can use me in this godless world. Hallelujah!

Now, I give all to Jesus Christ, my only friend—my honor, and my life, and my money, and all. And, you see, in the same time, Satan wanted to persecute me. But now, I fear nothing when I truly trust in the love of God (Romans 8:32–39).

Before, I was a slave of family, of society, of nation, of the world; I was a slave of my body, first of all. But now, thank the Lord, God has delivered me from all this. You see, a man cannot understand this. But anyone who is born of the Spirit of God only can shout "hallelujah" and say with the Apostle Paul, "Thanks be to God, who gives us the victory through our Lord Jesus Christ" (1 Corinthians 15:57, RSV).

Happy is anybody who can understand this! Anywhere and in all circumstances, in the affliction, in the darkness of this present life, in prison or in "death" there is always joy and happiness from the beloved Lord. I always thank the Lord for teaching me this lesson.

Now, I pray that my Lord will keep you all in his wonderful hands when we are watching and waiting for his return in the very short future. Amen.

On April 10, 1973, he wrote:

. . . I have heard that the political and economic situation in Cambodia has become worse but we thank the Lord for the mighty work of the Holy Spirit who has changed the hearts of many . . . I do believe the Lord has something for me to do for his glory and for the sake of his precious children there.

I thank him for changing my mind and my heart so wonderfully that the security of life I was looking for in Europe doesn't make sense to me any more. Matthew 10:39 speaks to me more clearly than ever before, Mr. Westergren. I still remember the Bible verse you gave me (Luke 9:62) eleven years ago when I left for France. The Lord touched my heart at that time and since then he has been my Friend, my Savior, my Lord, my Professor: my all . . . I wish I could find the right words to describe it. One day when we will be with Jesus before the throne of glory, we'll be speaking the heavenly language and it's better.

Please continue to pray for me that I will persevere to the end and that I may bear lasting fruit for Christ while I am still in the mortal body . . .

From a letter of May 26, 1973, when Chhirc was studying in Scotland:

. . . The Lord hasn't given me clear guidance
yet. I've been searching for his will and guidance
for many years, and I'm praying that this might
be his time to choose to answer me since I've
given my heart and life to him to use according
to his love for me. Please join me in this prayer.
God has laid a "heavy" burden on my heart
about the fate of his people in Cambodia . . .
May his holy name be glorified in a wonderful
way in that part of the world.

and July 3, 1973:

. . . I have learned a secret from Psalm 34: "I
will always thank the Lord; I will never stop
praising him."
   It is wonderful to thank the Lord and praise
his holy name in times of abundance as well as in
times of need. He puts us in every situation so
that he may teach us and transform us into his
likeness for his name's sake and for our own good.

   From such as these laymen and their countrymen
for whom they are willing to lay down their lives,
Christ is building his Church—and the Khmer Rouge
shall not prevail against it.
   Nevertheless, these Christians are invading Satan's
territory, and it's not all smooth sailing and
inspiration. The enemy forces are as active as they
ever were in opposing the gospel of Jesus Christ. One
Sunday right after the worship service at Sin Soum's
church, the district chief called all the villagers
together and forbade the Christians to meet in a
public gathering hereafter. It was a blatant
contradiction of the Constitution which allows
religious freedom, but there was no recourse
immediately. It was hard for the new believers and

their first reaction was to leave the village. But after reconsidering, they remained.

And there was the case of the man who had been director of the National Museum since 1966. He was relieved of his position even though he was the only man qualified in all of Cambodia in the field of archeology. The accusation? He and his wife were very active in the Mooneyham Crusade, "propagating a foreign religion; furthermore, the wife had gone to witness to the Museum personnel!" This man could not, therefore, be a faithful Cambodian at heart. In spite of his dismissal, his radiant face and evident inner joy revealed a ringing note of victory.

An upsurge of fervent and militant Buddhism was displayed in Buddhist youth rallies in which the young people were urged to oust the foreigners' religion.

An ongoing miracle was the marvelous protection of the Christians. Amazingly few fell prey to the bombing. One exception was a young member of Gene Hall's Bible class, the enthusiastic vice-president of the youth group. He had been a believer for just a little over a year. On a Saturday, he had said to Son Sonne, the head of the Bible Society, "If no one else will distribute literature, I will." Such was his concern for his own people and the necessity of disseminating the Word of God.

On Sunday morning this young fellow didn't show up at church. The pastor went on Sunday afternoon to see if he was sick, but a brother-in-law said, "No. We thought he was with you at the church since yesterday."

Monday morning an alert Christian identified the young man's bicycle through the keys still attached to it. What had happened? On Saturday at noon he had been the victim of a rocket that tore him limb from limb, leaving him so mutilated that he was scarcely recognizable. Later a secretary revealed that until 11:30 on Saturday morning, he had been in the office and had talked to her about Jesus, telling her that the only thing worth living for in all the world is Jesus. Through the death of this fine young Christian, his older brother came to know the Lord as his Savior.

Not always does God choose to deliver from danger and death; he accomplishes his purposes "whether by life or by death," in those who want to let God use them.

Cambodia has a host of laymen in this category. One is the musician who composed the Cambodian National Anthem, a man much decorated by his country. He has accepted Christ and is greatly enthused about writing Christian hymns and songs that will honor the Lord Jesus.

Some are doctors and they're witnessing to their Buddhist patients. One is the Justice of the Supreme Court.

Even a few years ago, such a thing would have been unthinkable. To the earliest missionaries it would have appeared sheer fantasy. Officialdom embracing Christianity! Officialdom had decreed, "There is no place in Cambodia for Christian missions"—but *God* had never said that.

Miraculous as it may seem, the day had arrived when a judge of the supreme court, a Khmer, took his place in the ranks of those who turned from Buddhism to serve the living Christ. This judge has said, "Since I met Dr. Stan Mooneyham and accepted Jesus Christ as my Savior, I have been very happy . . . I love my fellow Cambodians more since I know the Lord. I pray that they will find the peace I have found. My nation is far from God and much trouble comes because of this fact . . . I feel I have become a torch, and I want to go around lighting candles."

The man who might have become a monk

Whenever Cambodia and evangelism are mentioned, almost without exception, the man Son Sonne is somewhere at the heart of it.

He starts a Bible study in a new area. Thirteen people come. He asks them to invite their friends the next time. Over a hundred come and seventy-one accept Jesus as their Savior. Son Sonne goes to get permission from the district chief to hold church services. To his delight he finds that this man had been led to Christ and is thrilled to grant permission for the meetings.

This was in May 1974.

A problem: "With the churches now full, where are we going to put next month's new converts?"

"So many new Christians we can't begin to know them all by sight and by name."

These are the reports, and Son Sonne is a big part of these "problems."

Who is he, this ardent Christian who might have become a monk?

How much the church and the Khmer people would have missed if this man had gone through with his early training, and had followed his parents' hopes for his life. For eight years Son Sonne studied in a Buddhist temple; he has an uncle who is a high priest.

Searching for the truth, Son Sonne asked his uncle concerning sin, acts of merit, and heaven. His uncle told him he didn't have to become a monk to attain these things. So at the age of sixteen, Son Sonne left the temple. But God must have noted someone whose heart and mind was looking for answers to the questions of the ages.

In Phnom Penh where he went to find work, someone invited him to a service in the Evangelical Church. He received a Bible as he continued to attend, and the Book of Proverbs became especially meaningful to him. On Christmas Day, he and the young Chinese-Cambodian girl to whom he was engaged both put their faith in Jesus Christ. A visit to the Bible school at Ta Khmau sparked a longing that he and his wife might have the opportunity to study there. But Son Sonne had a good position and he didn't seriously consider attending Bible school.

It took adversity to nudge him. He was deeply shocked when one morning he was informed that his employer didn't need his services any longer. The reason? He had been bold in his witness to his fellow employees. That was for him just the beginning of persecution.

Jobs were hard to find and one, then two, three, and four months went by. One day he felt the Spirit of God reminding him about his Bible school aspirations.

Mrs. Merle Graven recalls their words the day Son Sonne and his wife arrived at the Bible school: "We have sold most of our possessions. I (Son Sonne) want to burn every bridge behind me so there will be no temptation to turn back."

Working in the church bookroom one day, Son Sonne was arrested and put in prison, the first to be prosecuted that year, 1965, because he would not stop preaching and teaching about Jesus Christ. He was in prison for three months.

After completing Bible school, Son Sonne could easily discern that losing his well-paid job had been the best thing that ever happened to him. (Except, of course, his uncle's advice that he need not be a monk in order to know the truth and to have his sins forgiven; that was probably the real turning point for Son Sonne.)

His ministry has been largely witnessing to his

people, starting small groups, and encouraging those who attended to bring more, branching out to new areas. Always a torch shedding light, the Light of the world.

At one period he was teaching three Bible classes a week and leading a fourth. Because of his many talents which he recognizes as from God, Son Sonne is invaluable in Cambodia where there have been so few outstanding Christian leaders.

Director of the United Bible Societies, he was also teaching a class in the English school sponsored by the church. During August 1972, he led thirty of his students to the Lord, then conducted Bible classes for several weeks to strengthen them. He is president of the Foreign Missionary Society of the Khmer Evangelical Church (C & MA), a member of the Relief Committee, chairman of the radio committee, and a member of the Mission translation committee. One of the finest of interpreters, he serves also in that capacity at special meetings and crusades. He frequently fills the pulpit on a Sunday.

An old lady sat up on the front at one such service. She leaned forward about a yard from the pastor's mouth so that she could hear clearly. At one point she spoke right up. "I'm a sinner. I want to know how I can know God and worship him."

The pastor? Son Sonne.

And to think he might have become a Buddhist monk!

These laymen you have met—a school teacher, an engineer, an Army major, a judge, and a businessman, all turned *God's* businessmen—are his VIPs. They represent others whose names likewise are recorded in God's eternal scroll.

13

The Last Message

"Good-bye, sir. See you in Phnom Penh."

A crackle—and the two-way radio between Bangkok and Phnom Penh fell silent.

"It is finished," said Col. Lieou Phin Oum, gesticulating in despair and forcing a smile. The Cambodian Armed Forces Attache, for days he had been the only source of news on the war for the journalists in Bangkok. Now the operator in his office covered the radio set with a newspaper and sat back dejected in his chair.

Five minutes before the radio died, the operator in Phnom Penh had reported demonstrations welcoming the Khmer Rouge, and the street scenes following the fall of Phnom Penh.

The Colonel's staff members stood by, silently staring at the equipment. There was no surprise

on their faces, only the deep sadness of the
moment and the uncertainty of the future.[1]

Finished? Cambodia finished?
Not in the spiritual sense!
"What God is doing in Cambodia is *present* tense."
Gene Hall's statement still rings true.
"It was a wrench for us to leave the people we
love. We've prayed with them, worshiped with them.
We've taught them and helped to bring them into a
relationship with the Lord Jesus.
"In another sense, though, there's a lot of rejoicing
for what God has done and is doing." Gene's face lit
up and he was suddenly far away with his beloved
Khmer people. Some seconds elapsed, then he
emphatically reiterated, "God's working in Phnom
Penh cannot be placed in the past tense; it is present
tense."
It's unquestionably harvest time in the "Golden
Land," as this part of the world was long known.
And it was a long time in coming. So long, in fact,
that anthropologists and missiologists are speculating
as to the explanation.
What sparked such phenomenal new life?
Phenomenal in that nearly half a century before, the
incredibly miniscule response would have driven
lesser souls than the earlier missionaries to board the
first boat home.
Commissioned to write about what God is doing in
Cambodia in the seventies, the same broad question
intrigued me. Probing with those who conceivably
had answers, people you have met on these pages, I
found certain factors consistently surfacing. In the
case of others it was a positive "*This* is it" as though

[1] *Voice of the Nation*, (daily newspaper) Bangkok, April 18, 1975.

what was being mentioned (e.g., laymen or literature) was the only feasible explanation.

What are the key factors to which knowledgeable, experienced men and women attribute God's merciful dealing with individuals in this nation? For Christ was never officially welcome in the bastion of Buddhism! We can at best make our educated guesses.

Was it God's ultimate vindication of the vision of a missionary statesman, C & MA's Dr. R. A. Jaffrey, who saw the high walls of Buddhism in a yet unreached country as just one more challenge? It's said of him that his missionary vision never rested. As soon as one country was occupied, he immediately began inquiring what lay beyond its borders. He then blocked off on a map this new territory and with a few colleagues prayed daily for an open door. Inevitably Cambodia stirred Dr. Jaffrey's missionary blood—and God's clock began to tick toward Cambodia's hour.

"Where there is no vision, the people perish," the Bible tells us (Proverbs 29:18, KJV).

But there *was* a vision for Cambodia. Can we discount it as a factor in what later happened?

We might consider next the part that prayer played.

Arthur Hammond's diary tells how three persons—quite unknown to each other and totally unaware that anyone else was doing so—committed themselves to pray one hour a day that Cambodia would be opened to Christian missions. This happened in the 1920s. They were an unlikely combination: one, a housewife in Chicago; the second, a cattle rancher on the western plains (he came to be known to the first missionaries as "the cowboy prayer partner"); and a woman in Florida. How did they know about Cambodia in those days? Dr. Jaffrey had written a pamphlet titled simply

Cambodia, and it had fallen into their hands.

At one point in his daily rendezvous with God, "the cowboy" felt a Presence in his room and heard a voice telling him to stop praying for the door to open to missionaries, and to begin to pray for the ones who were already there.

For half a century, there never failed to be a corps of people who prayed for the Khmer people, with almost never a story of success to egg them on. Each convert was like a rare orchid, plucked only after exhausting effort. Nevertheless they steadfastly prayed.

The following lines surely apply to those who were so faithfully supportive:

> Do you know what happened on that day
> When burdened for souls you tried to pray?
> Did you think you failed to touch the throne
> When your lips were dumb, your prayer a
>   groan?
> Over the sea in a hot, dry land
> A sower sowed with faltering hand.
> But, lo, in that hour refreshing came,
> God's servant spoke with a tongue of flame!
> And souls long steeped in a land of night
> Passed from gloom to marvelous light.
> Away from idols they turned to God,
> Finding their peace in Jesus' blood.
> 'Twas your faith had moved God's mighty hand.
> His blessings poured down in a desert land.
> —Author Unknown

More things *are* wrought by prayer than this world dreams of.

Prayer in itself would not have been enough. It rarely is, for God uses people. We could say in this instance that *prayer, people,* and *persistence* helped win the day. While seemingly not as aggressive as some missionaries are today, it may be that the self-effacing early missionaries were exactly the type God wanted to till Cambodia's soil for a later harvest. They quietly pursued their goals despite the often repeated ''you can't'' of officialdom.

We should also add *patience*. Apparently these were people who didn't go around digging up the seed to see why it wasn't sprouting faster. They could wait God's time so long as they knew they were doing his work in his will. We need to keep in mind that church-growth methodology, so strategic today, was hardly a theory a decade or so ago. They didn't have access to charts and graphs. Almost anything modern missions employ was not available—mass communication, speedy transportation, mechanization for producing written and visual presentation, etc.

Yet, not privileged to see a harvest, they doggedly persisted, these missionaries of the twenties through the sixties, nurturing and teaching the few converts from Buddhism.

Because The Christian and Missionary Alliance was the first Protestant mission in Cambodia, it follows that literature was a top priority right from the first. The phrase ''Publish glad tidings'' was a reality in the ministry of the Mission's founder, Dr. A. B. Simpson, in 1887. To supplement the preaching and teaching ministries, Dr. Simpson established a pattern for publication and distribution of Christ-honoring periodicals, books, and teaching materials.

As mentioned earlier, a prominent refugee confirmed the fact that the written word had been effective long before the open turning to Christ. This has been documented for me by Rev. Paul Ellison and his wife (Paul's parents had been the second missionary couple in Cambodia). ''The Cambodians always had literature," Paul stated. "They had read about Christ and many of them had made up their minds. It remained for circumstances to make the change possible."

The political situation, as it invariably does in any country, likewise affected the church in Cambodia.

Clifford Westergren shared with me this brief evaluation:

Church Periods

1923–33: opposition from the French government and from the Roman Catholics, resulting in restricted opportunities for the missionaries

1936–40: from past roots some new beginnings of growth and expansion

1941–46: no missionaries in the country—World War II

1947–57: a period of unlimited outreach—twenty-one new missionaries (there had been 16 in all from 1923–39)

1954: a milestone year—the year that the first complete Cambodian Bible was printed; the year that missionaries withdrew all pastoral subsidies. [Significantly, this was also the year that Cambodia regained her independence and became a member of the family of free nations]

1958–65: the Christian church emerges, though not yet officially recognized. The hard work of forty years is finally beginning to produce, but not yet the big harvest

1965–70: through nonrenewal of American visas, all U. S. personnel were phased out, a political move by Sihanouk. While it was a time of severe testing for the nationals, it also created an awareness in the churches,

1965–70   resulting in a new volume of prayer for
(cont.)   Cambodia. French missionary Daniel
              Boudreaux was God's strategist at this time;
              he was allowed to remain for two and a half
              years; then another French couple, Mr. and
              Mrs. Jean Fune, entered. Miss Nellie
              Guilbert, daughter of a Frenchman led to
              Christ by a Cambodian believer, had close
              ties with the royal family and freely
              witnessed. Her Royal Highness Princess
              Rasmi Norodom, who regards Nellie as one
              of her personal friends, once said to her,
              "Every time I think of you, I think of your
              God."

1970–75: In a 1970 coup that ousted the absent
              Prince Sihanouk (he was in Moscow at the
              time), Lon Nol came to power and the
              missionaries were permitted to return. At
              the invitation of the national church, a
              number did go back, and Christmas 1971
              saw the beginnings of the New Life upsurge
              in the Khmer Republic.

   Political freedom has to be one of the most
important factors in the spiritual explosion. Under
Sihanouk, the government made it as difficult as they
could for the church. Permission had to be obtained
for the printing of every item and then for
distributing it. There was a prohibition against the
missionaries' using a picture of any public building;
and the word for "queen" must never be used,
among other word restrictions. Nevertheless there
was a built-in advantage to all the "shalt-not's": when
approved, the printed item bore the government
stamp of approval. So, by patience and strict
adherence to the laws (reasonable or not), the

missionaries won respect. They would never bend to any form of bribery; they would take loss rather than jeopardize their position.

Some early friends of the missionaries became leaders in government. Some, behind the scenes, knowingly or unknowingly, advanced the Lord's work. A church permit had to be obtained from the highest level (like the Congress in the United States).

The political upheaval was, therefore, a catalyst. It made possible some of the things that were impossible in the Sihanouk regime. As previously mentioned, *Time* correspondent David Aikman quotes pastor Son Sonne as saying that *communism is sweeping away idolatry* (although in itself it is an undesirable thing).''

By "idolatry," of course, these pastors referred to Buddhism. Until the fall of Phnom Penh, it would appear that both Buddhism and communism were creating a wedge for Christianity, as the ranks of the believers swelled. Perhaps if there had been the same zeal on the part of Cambodian Christians in earlier years, God's clock would have struck for that country long before it did. For the converts in the seventies, the words of Jesus, "You are my witnesses," came to them with the impact of a telegram from heaven. They didn't have to be instructed to go out and tell others. It was the thing to do. Surely we have to agree that this kind of sharing greatly influenced the New Life movement.

The flight from their villages, traumatic as it must have been, released many from the traditions and mores that had bound the Cambodian for centuries. And in their sad plight they were now candidates for believing the Christian message. But was this, too, tied into God's special timing in his plan for the Khmer people? Other nations have been on the refugee march. What of the millions who streamed over the India border to escape the death penalty for the "crime" of being Hindus during "the bloody birth of Bangladesh"? Nowhere was unusual spiritual response recorded, though many Christians ministered to these pitiful people with deep compassion.

Was it the opportunity to break from tradition—a chance afforded by their fleeing from the patterned security—that helped open their minds?

Khmers are an indecisive people, as a group, says Clifford Westergren. They have not historically made up their own mind. But here they were jerked from the lifelong surroundings and strong religious ties, and some proved they *can* make a good decision.

As has already been shown, the Mooneyham crusades and other evangelistic endeavors were mightily used of God to bring Cambodians to Christ.

"Paradoxically," states David Aikman, "or perhaps not, the most visible Christian presence is not evangelism at all, but the humanitarian organizations responding to the crisis condition in Cambodia today. The second largest of these is World Vision. The most touching of their four-project program in Cambodia is the nutrition center for malnourished children in the unfinished shell of the Phnom Penh Cambodia Hotel."

Aikman cites the largest of these organizations, "Catholic Relief Services, who in their rice distribution and soup kitchens program feed an incredible 450,000 Cambodians a month."

The latter brings to mind my conversation with the American ambassador in Laos concerning this book. A piece of his advice was, "Find some leathery old priest and get his side of the story. I've been around Indochina," he assured me, then painted this word picture: "I've seen the refugees, milling, disorganized, panicky, totally without direction. And in this sea of confusion, I've noticed a pocket of people calm and orderly, seemingly knowing what they were doing. And in every instance, what has been the secret of this paradox? Somewhere right there is a leathery old Catholic priest moving like a father among them, spreading calm and order." (Incidentally, this ambassador is not himself a Catholic. I saw him first reading the Scripture in a Protestant church.)

Here he was objectively, from his own experience, giving credit where credit was due. Others will chronicle the dedicated efforts of the Catholic Relief Services, but I wanted to pay my passing tribute.

The need for compassionate reaching out to meet the human needs of the refugees and other Christians in dire straits around the world engaged many minds during the ten days of the Congress on World Evangelization in Lausanne. One speaker made his point succinctly in these words: "Jesus did not stuff the injured man's pockets full of tracts; he poured oil on his wounds."

Many instances of conversion have been reported among the Cambodians to whom such Christian compassion was shown.

Nor can we overlook the perhaps hitherto unknown unity among Christian workers. Suffering has no denomination; crisis, no creed. And these missionaries, doctors, nurses, and social workers were much too busy ministering in the name of Jesus to have time for divisive sectarianism. Cooperation was the order of the day.

In this connection, a warm instance of brotherly cooperation came to my attention the day I was leaving Hong Kong for home. Mr. Westergren shared it with me from a missionary's prayer letter he had just received. Tom Stebbins and his wife, evacuees, were en route to Manila. Stebbins presented their tickets at the airlines desk only to be informed that they could not proceed to their plane unless they had return tickets or had ongoing tickets beyond the Philippines. Even while they were pondering their dilemma, for they had neither return nor ongoing tickets, nor did they have the funds to purchase them, a hand reached from behind them and a friendly voice said, "Here, take my credit card and get your tickets."

It was Bob Pierce.

By chance he was at the airport when I was waiting for my flight and I told him how the incident had warmed my own heart. "The Lord just told me to take that particular flight that day," he explained.

God has a way of having the right people at the right place at the right time—if they are sensitive to his still, small voice.

We could go on and on evaluating and enumerating, and we would never quite satisfy ourselves or each other as to what sparked the spiritual flame in the Khmer Republic, and kept it burning.

In summary, we might consider this list:

The caliber of the first missionaries
Consistent prayer
Literature
Persecution and trial
Zealous laymen and pastors
Political upheaval
Evangelistic crusades
Auxiliary personnel
Disillusionment with Buddhism

Christian compassion demonstrated in a practical
    manner
God giving people a heart to believe

Towering in importance above everything we can
think of or rationalize is the shining truth of the
sovereignty of God. The Almighty has a plan—for the
individual and for nations. He is sorting out the
pieces man jerks out of place in his fumbling and his
wars. And lest we might be tempted to question the
uprooting, the dismal plight of the refugees, and their
bleak future, we can remind ourselves of another
question: "Shall not the Judge of all the earth do
right?" (Genesis 18:25, RSV).

Ultimately, the key factor is, in my opinion, that
God so loves man that he can bring together the
needed circumstances. And if this takes a long time,
he can wait, even for a people who for long centuries
denied him.

But when they *did* turn—!

Perhaps it was best enunciated by a Khmer general
who was heard to say, "I *can't* leave; the Christians
would overrun the city." (Shades of Acts 17:6?)

"No success," the governor had predicted. Oh,
but he couldn't see that far ahead!

"It is finished," said the Cambodian official.

"It is finished," declared another from a
cross—and his words have echoed down the corridors
of time. They ring today. For this was not his last
message. He is the living Christ who has brought new
life and hope to suffering Cambodia.

Epilogue

What about Cambodia today?

What happened to the Khmer Republic following the fall of Phnom Penh on April 17, 1975?

At the time of this writing, virtually nothing is known for certain.

It's as if the world press had locked a door and tossed away the key. But no. They have published the meager "news" available to them—have reported the incredible—the almost mystical—happenings that have Asia watchers puzzled.

May 9, in an article datelined Bangkok, *The Hong Kong Standard* wrote:

Under a blanket of total silence, Cambodia is now being "purified."

The Red Khmer forces which took over the country on April 17 had long ago prepared a plan to move millions of inhabitants into liberated zones where they would be instilled with the spirit of service in the revolution.

And as the revolution started from zero, so will the people of Kampuchea (Cambodia).

The same day, and from the same source, Bangkok, *The Honolulu Advertiser*'s grim black headlines screamed,

CAMBODIAN CAPITAL
NOW A GHOST TOWN

Foreign refugees evacuated from Cambodia said the Khmer Rouge ordered the mass exodus as a first step to building a new Communist order in Cambodia.

In Phnom Penh, the pullout extended to hospitals swollen with wounded. Patients were trundled down roads in hospital beds to join the procession into the countryside. . . .

The 1,249 foreign refugees who made a difficult, three-day truck trip along war-battered roads from Phnom Penh to the Thai border, said Phnom Penh appeared to be a ghost town.

Cambodian refugees forced out of Phnom Penh were believed to have been sent back to their home towns. [As I read this I remembered the scattering of the early Christians, driven out of Jerusalem. And I recalled that scores of Cambodian students, new Christians, had expressed their fervent hope of getting back to their villages with the gospel of the Living Christ. *How many made it?* I wonder.] The city's natives were thought to have been sent to the countryside for "weeding out" by the Khmer Rouge.

Again quoting the *Hong Kong Standard:*

> "They have gone to liberated areas organized to receive them. Later, they will return to their homes, clean," journalists in the evacuation convoy were told. They will return with no useless belongings, to start their life from zero, free of the artificial needs of the Western world which was never theirs. That is the Red Khmer plan.

August 12 the *Los Angeles Times* carried a story by its staff writer, Robert S. Elegant.

> WASHINGTON—A deliberately faceless regime, in an audacious display of social engineering, is transforming Cambodia, a nation of 7 million people, into a vast, isolated plantation. . . .
>
> The populace, at great cost in lives and suffering has been set to clearing and cultivating the land. Almost all internal and external communications have been severed by the new "hermit kingdom."
>
> The shadowy leadership is known only as ANGKA, an acronym best translated as "the organization." No outsiders and few Cambodians know what, or where, ANGKA is.
>
> "The new Cambodian government—insofar as it exists—has mounted a quasi-religious campaign to wipe out all 'evil' by forcibly returning the entire populace to a primeval state of pastoral innocence" observed a senior Washington analyst. "Men and women have been stripped not only of names but of personal identity. It's like George Orwell's 1984 rewritten by Franz Kafka . . . who denied his characters (and

readers) almost all knowledge of the powers that perpetrated gross indignities and cruelties upon them.''

Soaring idealism and financial ruthlessness have combined to tell not only the outside world but the 20th century to get out of Cambodia. Historians find uncanny parallels with the still unexplained exodus from the capital of Angkor in the late middle ages that abruptly ended the high period of indigenous Cambodian civilization.

The tale of a nation that has obsessively turned its back on the modern world was pieced together in Asia, New York and Washington. It is necessarily incomplete because information is sparse and because there is, by design, so little to tell.

The key word in the new Cambodian lexicon is ''elimination.''

First to go were the cities, historically and semantically the cradles of civilization;

ANGKA has also eliminated names and personalities; men and women alike are called ''comrade'';

Money has been eliminated since ''the organization'' sees neither need nor justification for even barter trade.

Also eliminated have been:

—the printed and broadcast word after a two-week destruction by bonfire of literature, official records, radios and television sets in Phnom Penh.

—modern machinery, including motor vehicles as stocks of gasoline are used up; the temples and clergy of a devoutly Buddhist nation;

—communication between different parts of

the country and with the outside world;

—all class distinctions, private wills and property;

—recognizable individual personalities within the anonymous government, if not formal government itself.

The fundamentalist new leadership has not even bothered to claim two Air Camboge planes standing on the tarmac at Bangkok's Dom Muang Airport.

Some estimates hold that several hundred thousand have already died and an additional 500,000 will die by the end of the year (1975) if present practices are not radically altered and Cambodia does not receive substantial supplies of food from abroad.

Cholera, malaria, and other endemic diseases reportedly are killing thousands, with dehydration and starvation killing more. An entire social class, largely drawn from the former cities, is thus being eliminated. . . .

Undersecretary of State Philip C. Habib told Congress in Washington last month [July 1975] that the Cambodian situation involves "substantial killings" and "goes far beyond the bounds of normal decency."

". . . ANGKA would clearly prefer to exclude all foreign influences while it pursues its vision of recreating a classless, pastoral paradise untroubled by the tumultuous outside world.

This, then, is all that is known of the new Cambodia.

But a nation is its people wherever they are on the face of the earth. And Cambodians, fleeing for their lives from this ruthless regime, are found in many countries today. Thousands of refugees are in no way part of this "strange, faceless society." To be sure, they are tragically bereft of family members and friends. And, if the supposition of at least one missionary, Merle Graven, is correct, many of the Christians they left behind in Cambodia have, to quote this missionary, "exchanged their cross for a crown."

"How does one equate the tragedy that is Cambodia and its hapless refugees scattered throughout the world with God's promise that when he 'opens a door, no man can shut it'?" This is a question that has engaged missionary Gene Hall. He explains, "Cambodia had been the object of God's grace in an unusual way since 1970. During this time of war the church grew rapidly. Churches in Phnom Penh increased from three to twenty-nine. The Sunday attendance rose from 300 to 4000. A new Christian hospital was completed and ready for opening. All signals were 'go' for 1975—and then the country fell.

"Has God slipped up and failed his Word? Let us take a look at some of the reports from missionaries who are still working among Cambodians these days. Jimmy Rim, a Korean, reports that 600 Cambodians have turned to Christ in a refugee camp in South Thailand. In Northeast Thailand John Ellison has led over a hundred refugees to Christ. Norman and Marie Ens saw twenty-one come to Christ in their home in Bangkok. Merle Graven recently spoke in the Indiantown Gap refugee center and 123 responded to the invitation to receive Christ. Eight hundred conversions are reported on Guam. At Camp Pendleton 118 persons have accepted Christ, and seventy-three of these have followed the Lord in baptism. Andrew Way of the Overseas Missionary

Fellowship is training 170 for baptism in South Thailand. Within a period of approximately three months nearly 1000 have made decisions for Christ.

"Many of these refugees began their search for God while fleeing to safety," explains Mr. Hall.

While visiting at Camp Pendleton, I have personally heard a number of these new Christians tell of their harrowing experiences as they sought to escape and subsequently came to know Jesus Christ.

Words can scarcely describe what has been and is still going on, spiritually, in the refugee camps in the United States and elsewhere. On my first visit to Camp Pendleton, properly credentialed by the Press division there, and given a Marine escort for the day, I interviewed individual refugees, some who speak English and others through an interpreter. I attended an English class conducted by vivacious, highly competent Rose Ellen Chancey, OMF missionary who had worked with the C & MA in Phnom Penh. It was an experience for me *and my escort* to be in on this. The people were so intent on learning and the teacher had such a way of relating to them and really imparting the language. Later, we went to the Bible class in the same tent and again there was this 100 percent attention to the vitally presented lesson. But between these two sessions was the ultimate! I was seated in the small C & MA office in a Quonset building with Rose Ellen Chancey and Mrs. Lee Bendell, wife of the Marine colonel who had graciously arranged press privileges for me at Camp Pendleton. A knock at the door, Rose Ellen's "Come in," and a young man entered. He had come by appointment to accept Jesus as his Savior. He was twenty-seven and had been an officer in the Cambodian Navy. At the missionary's request he shared his story.

"I heard from others that the Khmer Rouge were killing the officers, and I didn't want to get killed."

One of a group of 700 in a three ship convoy, he was on the seas from April 18 to May 17. They went from port to port and were refused admittance by five countries. At one port in Malaysia, an American ambassador arranged for food and other necessities for the desperate voyagers and suggested they try the Philippines. There, too, the chances looked bleak until they were advised to strike their Cambodian flag and raise a United States flag.

From Clark Air Base, this young man, Mr. Cheang Yuan, had been brought to Camp Pendleton. There he followed some of his countrymen to a tent where, he learned, the Bible was being taught. "After a few days," he related, "I began to think that these words of Jesus were *truth*."

"Had you ever studied the Bible in Cambodia?" the missionary asked him.

He answered, No, then added, "When I heard the stories of Jesus, I began to feel happier. I have hope that God will help me and let me see my family again. I *will* see them again. *I believe* that!"

He had obtained a paperback New Testament and already—it was now two weeks since he had first heard of Jesus—his New Testament was all marked up as if he were a veteran Bible conference attender.

In the manner that I had learned is characteristic of the Cambodians when they have heard the gospel and believed, he had made this appointment with the missionary to accept Jesus. Carefully, Rose Ellen took him through the Scriptures pertaining to sin, repentance, God's forgiveness, Christ's death and resurrection. And earnestly he traced it in his own New Testament.

"Why did you not ask Jesus to come into your

heart?'' asked the missionary (he was obviously ready). I'll always hear this young Cambodian's reply. Very simply and directly he said, "I do not know how to pray to your Jesus."

Then, with the utmost courtesy he indicated the colonel's wife and myself (our Marine escort was just outside the door) and said, "If the ladies do not mind, I want to receive Jesus *right now*."

The next few moments were too holy for tape recorder or camera. The recording angel was busy doing his work and there was rejoicing in heaven.

Meeting this new Christian on my next trip to the camp was just like greeting a relative (as indeed he is: a brother in Christ). In the meantime he had proven a great help to the missionaries (Mr. Gene Hall had arrived in the interim) and the young man was being discipled and strengthened in his faith before moving out. He had a sponsor and a home to go to. It was good news to me that these new Christians were being sponsored, that many of them did have a place to go as soon as the camp procedures were completed.

Again, in the same Quonset office, this time with Gene Hall, I met a number of men who shared their experiences as refugees fleeing the terror in their homeland, then finding peace in Jesus Christ as they came to the safety of a U. S. refugee camp.

As I had before, I attended the Bible study at 4 P.M. in the tent set aside for classes. When we arrived another group was just finishing a session. As some of us sat waiting for "our" class to begin, a young American girl who had been assisting in the previous class began to make her way to the back exit of the tent. She smiled and greeted the various Cambodians as she passed, then she sat down on an end seat to speak with someone. Hardly had she positioned herself on the bench than two or three people surrounding her asked, almost in unison and with big smiles, "Are you a *Christian?*"

"Oh, ye-es," she responded with her own broad smile.

"How long?" was the next piece of information these new Christians wanted to know. "About three years," she told them. Then voices buzzed, the dark-eyed, dark haired Cambodians leaning across the aisle and from in front and behind the blond American fellow-Christian. "Two months." "One week." "Three weeks." "Since I came to this camp." "Since I heard about the Living Jesus." For a few minutes the "Birthday" testimonies swirled. It was worth driving from Pasadena to Camp Pendleton just for those precious moments. (I think the first few eons in heaven might be something like this.)

Then it was time for the singing. I thought as I sat in that tent with its backless benches, *What would I have to sing about if I were in the shoes of these who sat with me there? They had fled from a living nightmare—had left, many of them, the people dearest to them on earth—they were without a home, and whether sponsored or not, their future was at best uncertain.*

I wasn't left to wonder what *they* would sing about and how can I ever forget it?

> God is so good; God is so good
> God is so good; He's so good to me.

They sang and sang, adding "I praise His Name," and a variety of other lines of praise. Leading them, Gene Hall's face positively shone. They praised the Lord in Cambodian hymns, too, then Gene, using the chalkboard, taught them the chorus of "How Great Thou Art," in *English.* I could sing that with them.

The Bible studies are lively with much

participation, group reading of the verses and response to the speaker's questions (by contrast with our rhetorical process which doesn't necessarily engage our minds).

The Bible study was over. The benediction had been given in Cambodian. We were ready to leave, when a young man at the back of the tent stood up and said, "I have a testimony." Mr. Hall waved him up to the front of the tent. How I deplored that Tower of Babel fiasco that kept me from being able to know what he said. But that didn't prevent my sensing it, and the facts were filled in for me later by Mr. Hall.

The man's testimony? He held up a letter. The big news in it was that a friend to whom he had witnessed and who had been sponsored out of the camp was going to church with his sponsor and was beginning to believe in Jesus. The man's joy was both evident and infectious. Everyone applauded. But that was just part of his testimony for the day. He explained that ever since he'd been at Pendleton, "I have not had even one coin in my pocket. It was embarrassing when someone asked me to go with him (to a refugee commissary in another area). I was ashamed. I asked God to help me with this problem and—" he reached into another envelope and with a smile that would give the sun competition, he held up three U. S. bills—one $10 and two $20 bills. "God answered my prayer; he sent this money—" His voice was drowned in another round of applause. It was as if each one in the tent had received a windfall.

But not yet could I start for home. Gene Hall came to me as the people were dispersing. "Can you wait a little while, Jeanette?" he asked. "There's a young man who wants to receive Jesus." A curtain of holiness dropped on that corner of the tent. Earnest men and women sat in prayer while Gene dealt with another Cambodian whose name was recorded that August afternoon in the Lamb's Book of Life.

Seeing these believers and reading and hearing of others just like them, I find myself pondering often the secret of their abounding joy and peace. Does God, I wonder, have a special brand of peace and joy for those who are totally dependent on him? It would appear to be so. Or—which is more likely—is it that the rest of us settle for a lesser, a kind of Brand X, and mix it with our own self-sufficiency—for we are not homeless refugees?

They believe in sharing their good things, these refugees.

Gene Hall tells of the day a busload of new Christians was transported to the swimming pool at Camp Pendleton for a baptismal ceremony. (Come to think of it, isn't there an ironic twist to all this: *Bible studies, baptisms.* What would the Madalyn O'Hare devotees do about this, in a United States Marine facility!) But back to the busload of refugees. When the baptismal service was over and the men and women had returned to the bus, the driver asked Mr. Hall if he would have them sing their hymns on the way back to their area. Gene had driven his own car. So it was not at his instigation the Christians had sung. They were sharing out of the fullness of their own hearts. So they sang their way back again, and a few days later the Marine indicated his own interest in the gospel of Jesus Christ.

A heartwarming incident points up the spirit of the Marines toward the refugees. In preparation for the arrival of the first group, the Marines assigned to this duty worked around the clock for days, including all day Saturday. They drove off when the task was completed, "after working like dogs," as was reported to me. But late Saturday night a group of volunteers came back in a truck and unloaded and put up a special tent. "What's it for?" a Marine onlooker asked. And this was the answer he got. "Tomorrow's Sunday, and maybe some of these refugees will want to worship," and the men proceeded to unload benches and a table.

A worship and Communion service crowned the day of the baptisms. Reporting on it, Mr. Hall said, "We read from the Gospel of John, chapters 18, 19, and 20; for 90 percent of the 125 present it was the first time they were reading these entire chapters as it was their very first Communion service. We read all together, aloud, through the betrayal, the trial, the scourging, the mocking; we read of the crucifixion and the burial of Jesus. Then we came to chapter 20. And as we read of the resurrection of Christ and of his appearances to his own people, something began to build up in that tent—like a vibrating, electric spirit. And when we reached the end of our reading it was like being at the finish line and cheering the victor. These Cambodians applauded and applauded Jesus Christ for his supreme victory of life over death. There was in it a feeling that each one present (for all had put their faith in Jesus) had been a victor in a contest. I'll never forget it—and I may never be in such a meeting again."

Because the Communion service was a new thing to so many, Mr. Hall briefed them on holding the elements until all had been served.

"This Communion service was also unlike any I'd ever been in," said Gene Hall. "To the Cambodian with his background of god/king worship, it would be unthinkable to sit in the presence of deity (or any honored personage). In this service they were worshiping *Jesus*. So, as the bread was offered to the first one, he rose to his feet, then clasping his upheld hands in a gesture of honor, he prayed. And not till then did he take the bread. In turn, each person did this. Some prayed silently; others openly praised the Lord. And a kind of glory seemed to fill that tent.

"Let us praise the Lord, praise the Lord," they sang from full hearts.

What lies ahead for these Christian refugees? For Cambodians wherever they are?

Only God knows. And he *does* know.

To us who have shared their experiences through these pages there comes a responsibility to care what becomes of them, to pray, and in practical ways as God leads us, to show that we care.